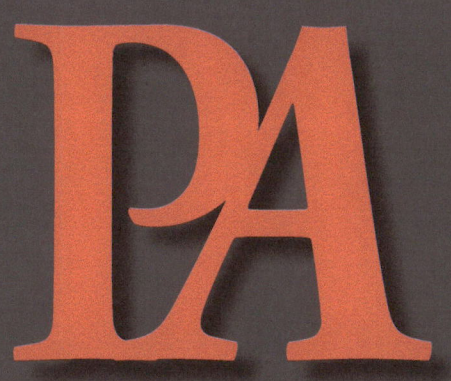

PA#55, May 2014
Publisher/Creator/Designer Didi Menendez
a publication of GOSS183
www.poetsandartists.com
Copyright PoetsArtists Contributors
Submission guidelines may be found on the web site.
Available in print and digital formats.

Curated by Sergio Gomez

contributors

Jennifer Balkan
Liz Mares
Miranda Graham
Victoria Selbach
Aneka Ingold
Spencer Corbett
Cesar Santos
Ali Cavanaugh
Ryan Shultz
Matthew Cherry
William Lazos
Aleksander Betko
Riva Lehrer
Terry Adams
Richard Frost
ShirrStone Shelter
Debra Livingston
Jamilah Adebesin Mason
James Needham

RAW Beauty examines the human figure in its states of change. In a culture that glorifies physical perfection and often creates deceiving images of beauty, the works in this issue explore the opposite side of accepted physical perfection. The works were selected for their ability to embody the true stages of change in the human form. From facial wrinkles that come with age to physical irregularities, these works will give justice and a humanized platform to an often hidden beauty that exists in the other side of our television screen. Each work elevates the raw beauty of the human form without the deceiving glamour of a make-up artist or a digitally manipulated image. RAW celebrates the beauty of the human form often found in the ordinary aspects of our constant states of change.

Sergio Gomez

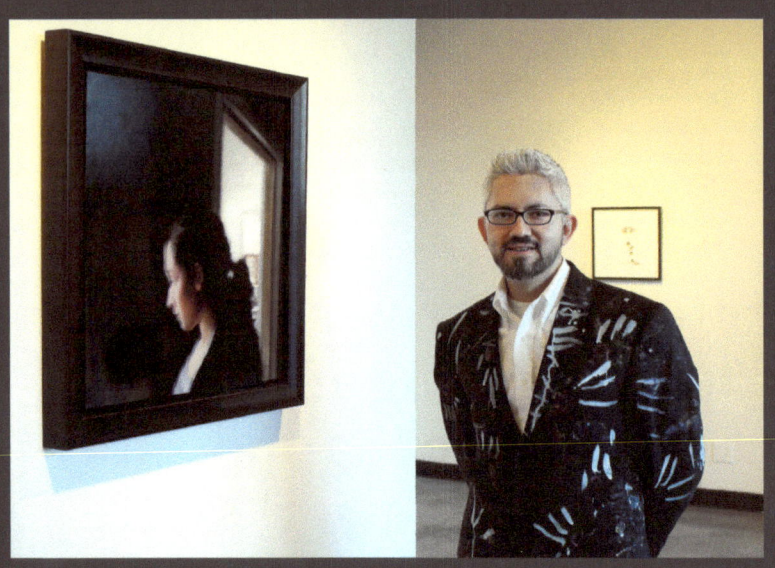

Sergio Gomez is a Chicago based visual artist. He received a Master of Fine Arts degree from Northern Illinois University. As an art student at Governors State University, Sergio was recipient of the Lincoln Laureate Medallion Award given by the Lincoln Academy and former Governor of Illinois Mr. Jim Edgar. Sergio's work has been subject of solo exhibitions in the United States, Italy and Vienna. He has participated in numerous group exhibitions in Spain, Sweden, Mexico and the US. His work can be found in private and public collections of the National Museum of Mexican Art, Brauer Art Museum, and the MIIT Museo Internazionale Italia Arte among others.

The human form is the most important element in Sergio's work and it exists as an anonymous representation of the self. The figure dominates the work and it is depicted as a shadow, aura, ghost or energy light. Sergio is interested in the human and spiritual experience throughout the cycles of life.

Presently, Sergio Gomez is the Director of Exhibitions at the Zhou B. Art Center, owner & director of 33 Contemporary Gallery, contributor for Italia Arte Magazine, founder of VisualArtToday.com; a curated online exhibition space for international contemporary art. In addition, Sergio is an accomplished graphic designer, Art/Design faculty at South Suburban College, Creative Consultant for Idea Seat Marketing and Advertising and co-founder of 3C Wear LLC.

As a curator, Sergio has organized numerous important exhibitions such as "The National Self-Portrait Exhibition", "Get Real: New Figurative Realism in Chicago" "CelebrARTE", "Chicago's Twelve", "Chicago's Twelve at Garfield Park Conservatory", "Style Bombing" and the "National Wet Paint Biannual MFA Exhibition" which has become a catalyst for emerging painters across the country. Additionally, Sergio has established international art collaborations in Italy, Austria, Mexico, Spain, Chile and China.

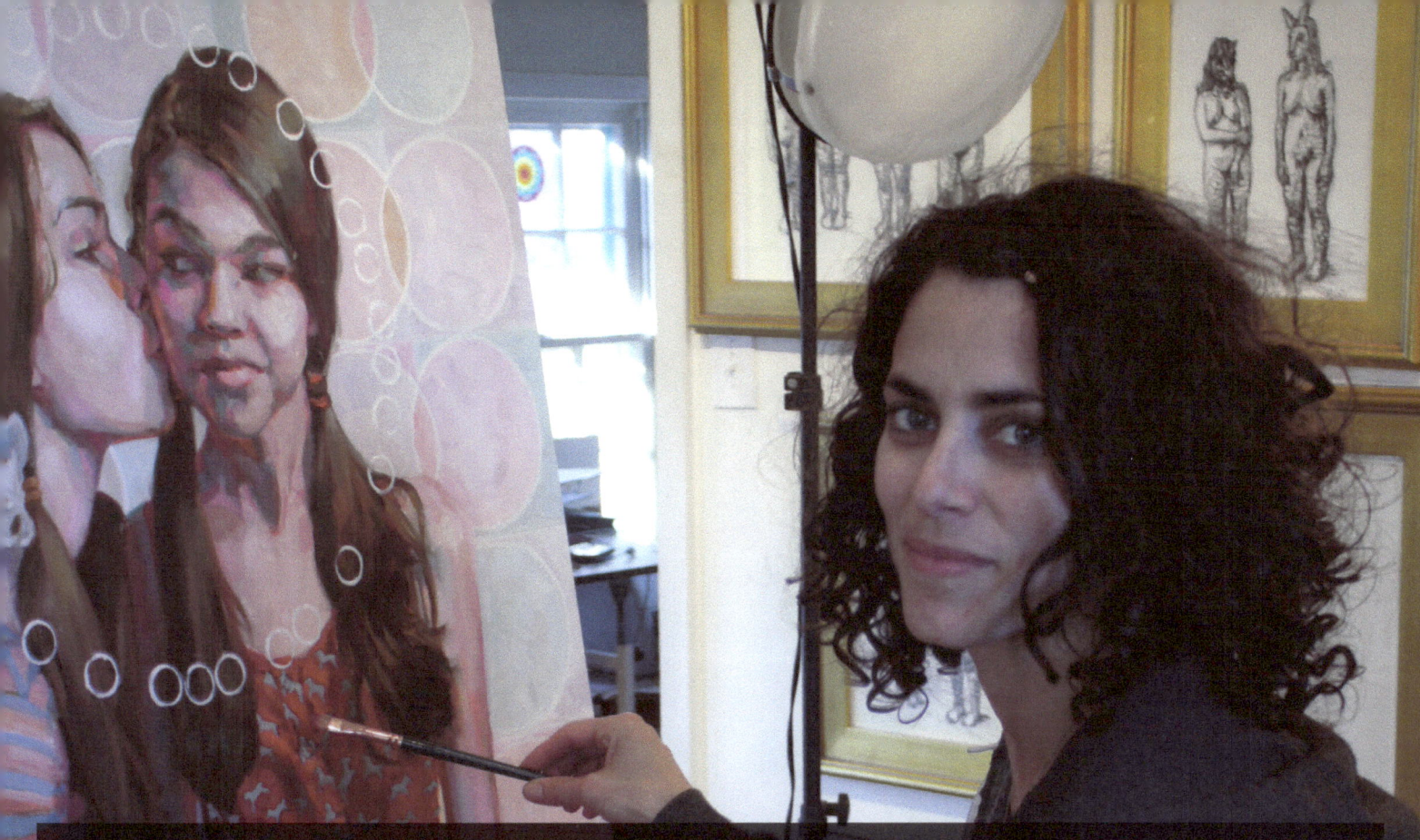

Although Jennifer Balkan had drawn all her life, she didn't embrace her passion to paint until 2001. Jennifer grew up in one of the countless suburbs of New Jersey in between the Holland Tunnel and the Jersey Shore which spawned an obsession with the Ferris wheel, arcade games, funnel cake and all other Boardwalk decadence. She studied behavioral neuroscience at Lehigh University in Pennsylvania. After graduation, Jennifer worked her way out west to Seattle after a brief stay in Boulder where she worked in a rat lab and found people not afraid to speak their minds. In Seattle, Jennifer worked serving the mentally ill and developmentally disabled population. From Seattle, she was pulled to Austin to study Latin American sociology at the University of Texas. Jennifer attained her Ph.D. in 2001 after conducting anthropological fieldwork on human migration in Chiapas, Mexico in 1999. Although her experience in Mexico was rich, she longed for artistic creativity. In 2002, Jennifer quit her full-time job doing social scientific research and threw herself into oil painting and now paints fervently. She has taken art classes at Laguna Gloria Art School in Austin, the Austin Fine Arts School and at the Art Students League in Denver. She currently paints full-time and teaches painting classes to groups in her studio.

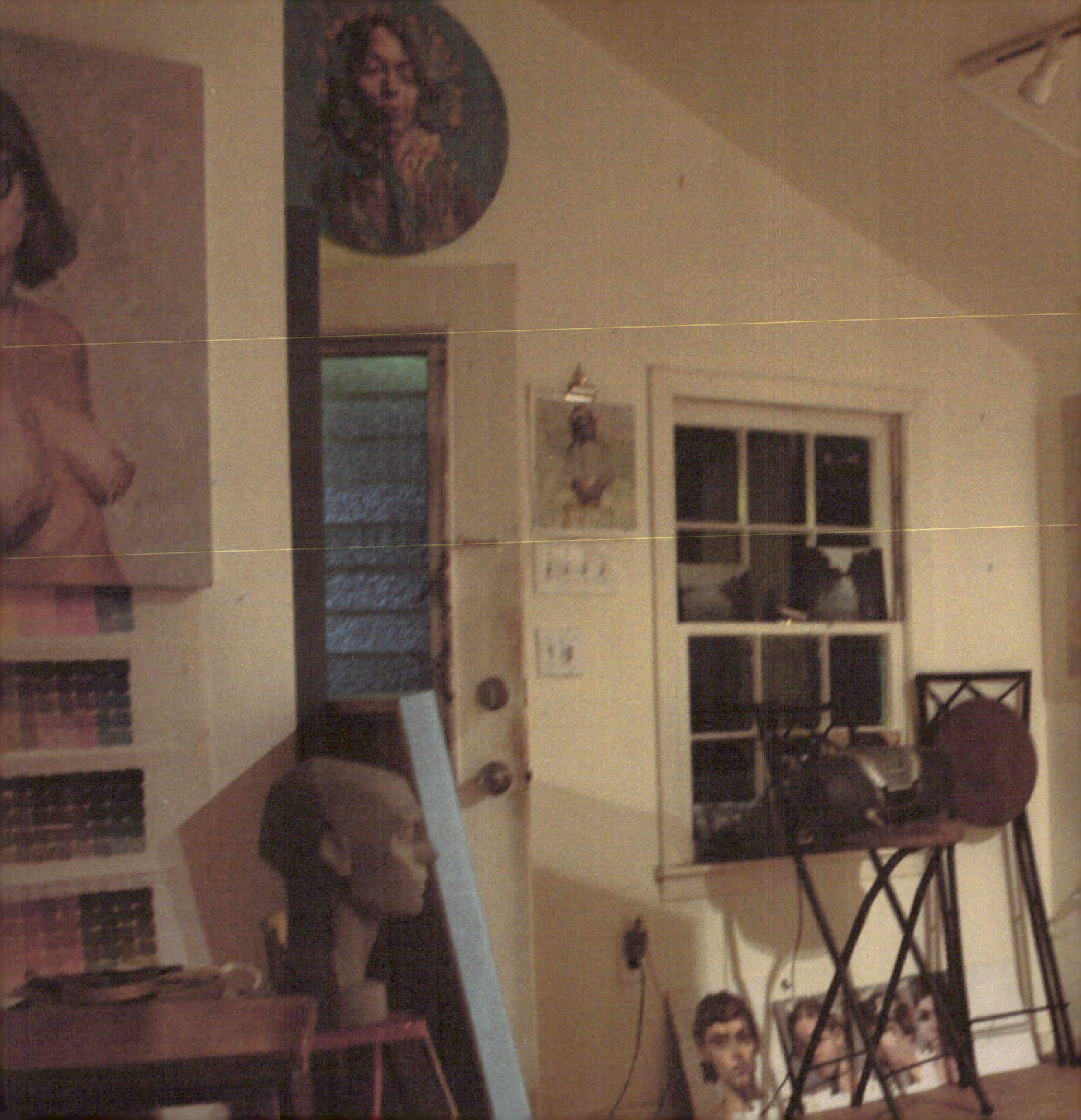

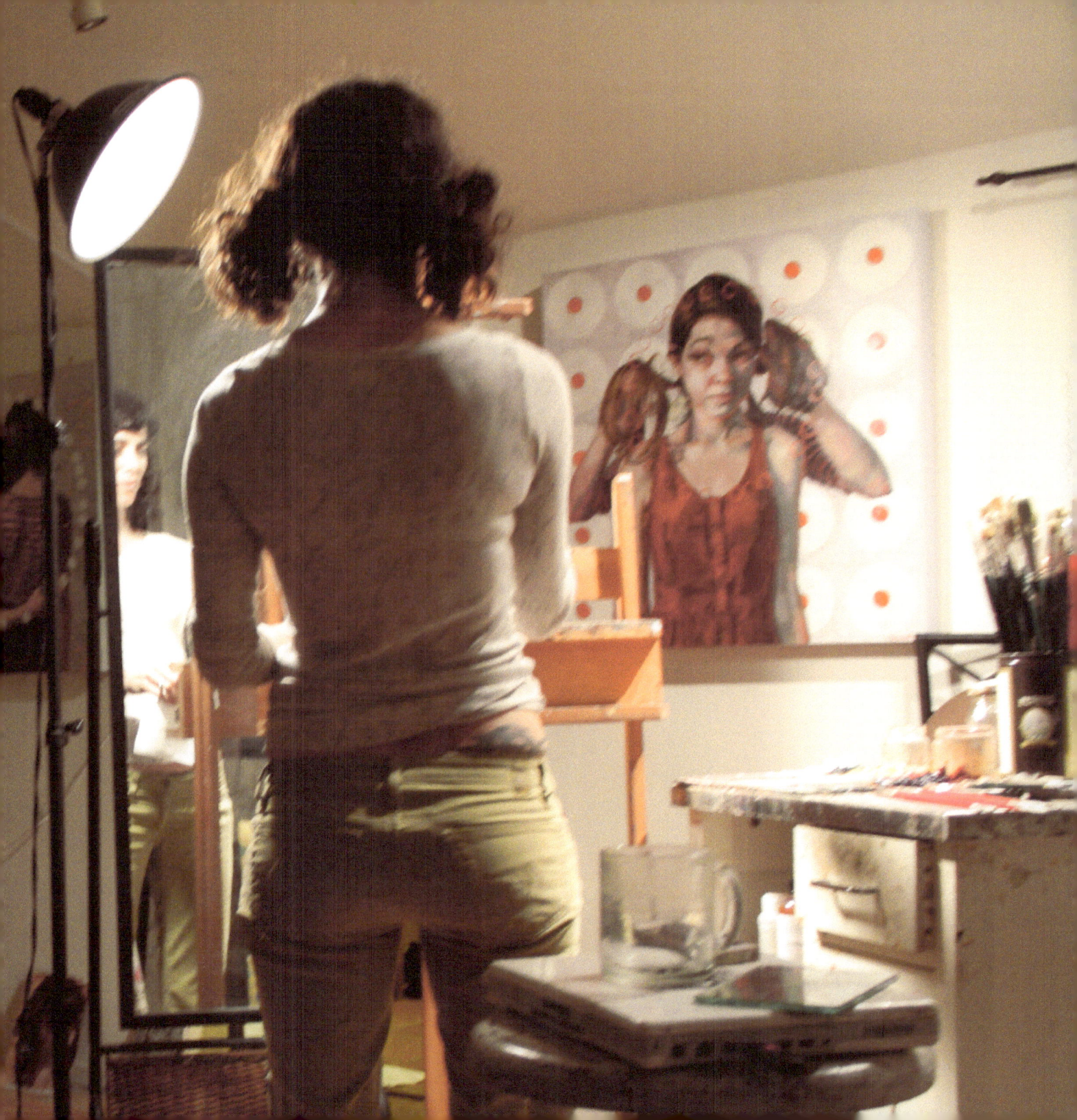

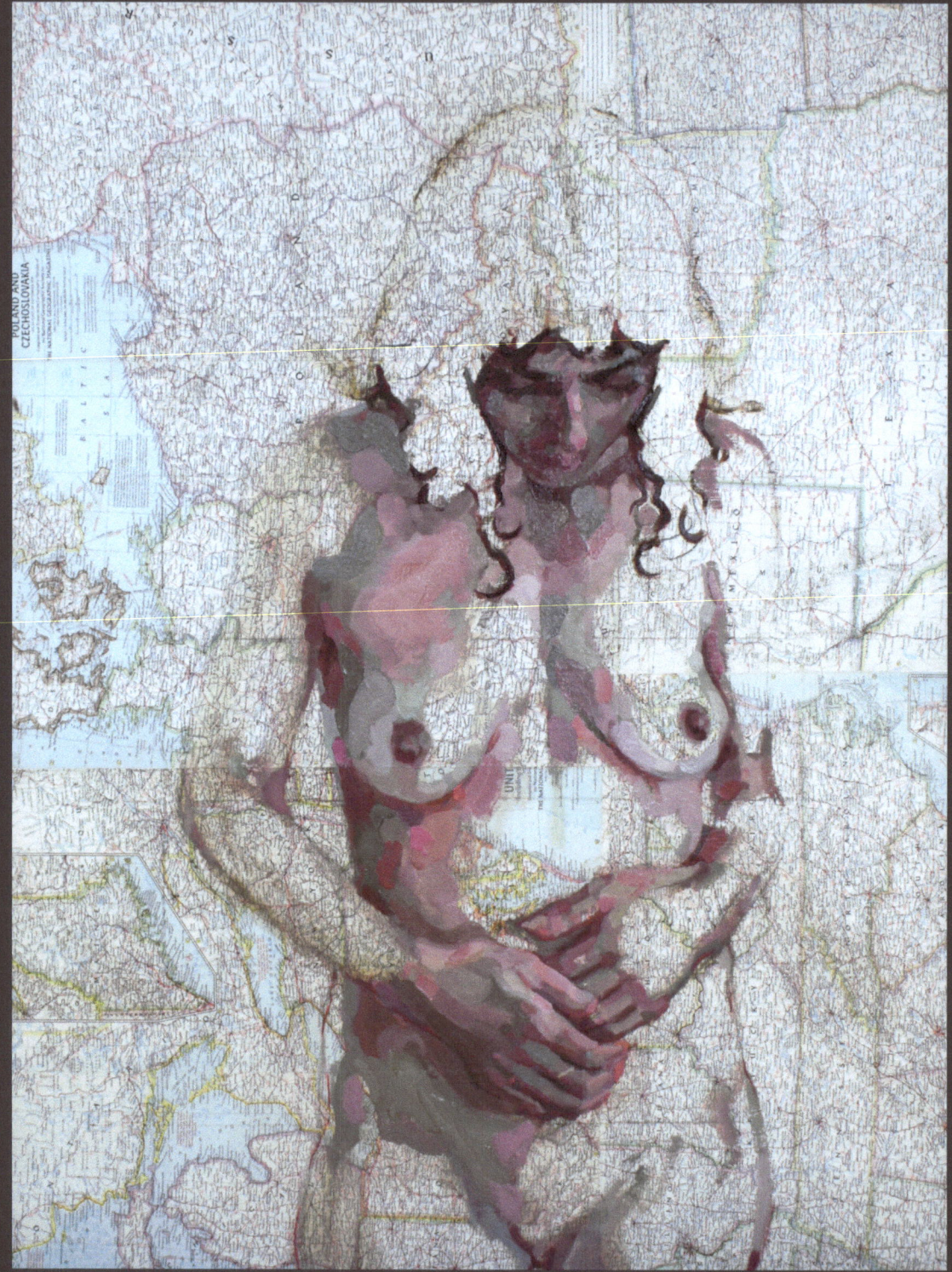

Jennifer
Balkan

My topography
oil on map fragments
mounted on wood
42x30 inches

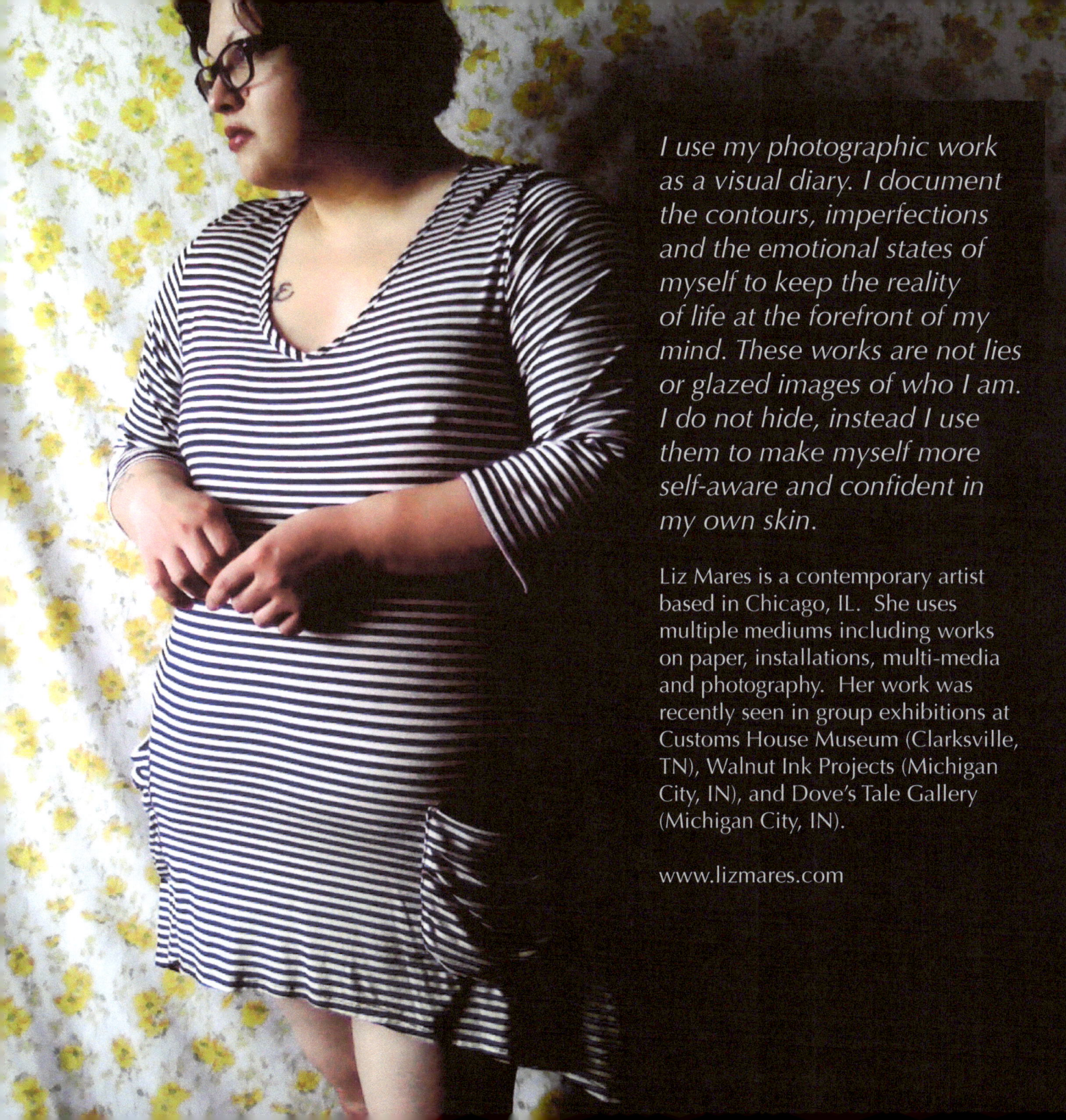

I use my photographic work as a visual diary. I document the contours, imperfections and the emotional states of myself to keep the reality of life at the forefront of my mind. These works are not lies or glazed images of who I am. I do not hide, instead I use them to make myself more self-aware and confident in my own skin.

Liz Mares is a contemporary artist based in Chicago, IL. She uses multiple mediums including works on paper, installations, multi-media and photography. Her work was recently seen in group exhibitions at Customs House Museum (Clarksville, TN), Walnut Ink Projects (Michigan City, IN), and Dove's Tale Gallery (Michigan City, IN).

www.lizmares.com

Liz Mares

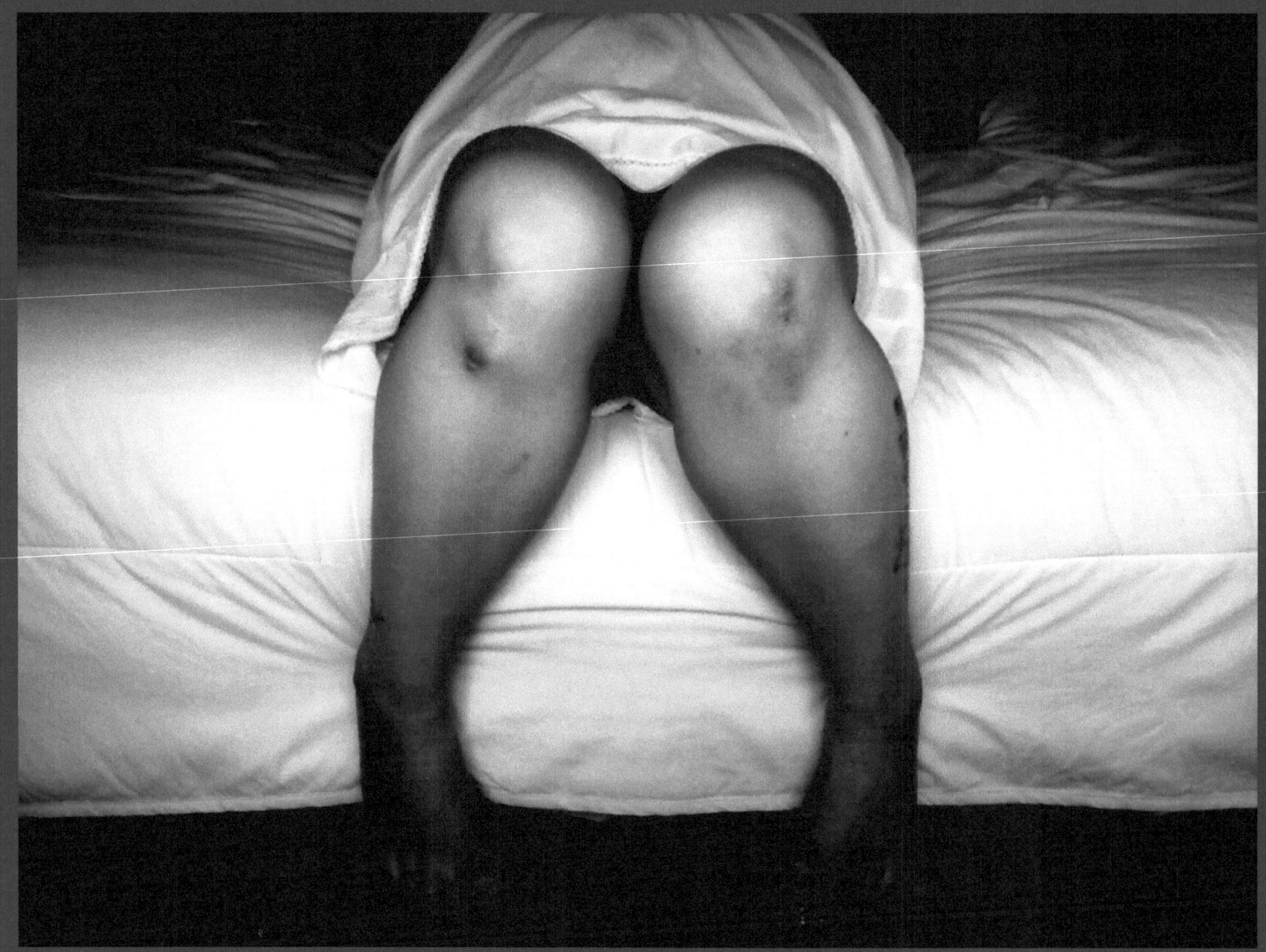

Disorder
Laptop Generated Image
7x5 inches

PA #55 Curated by Sergio Gomez May 2014

Miranda Graham

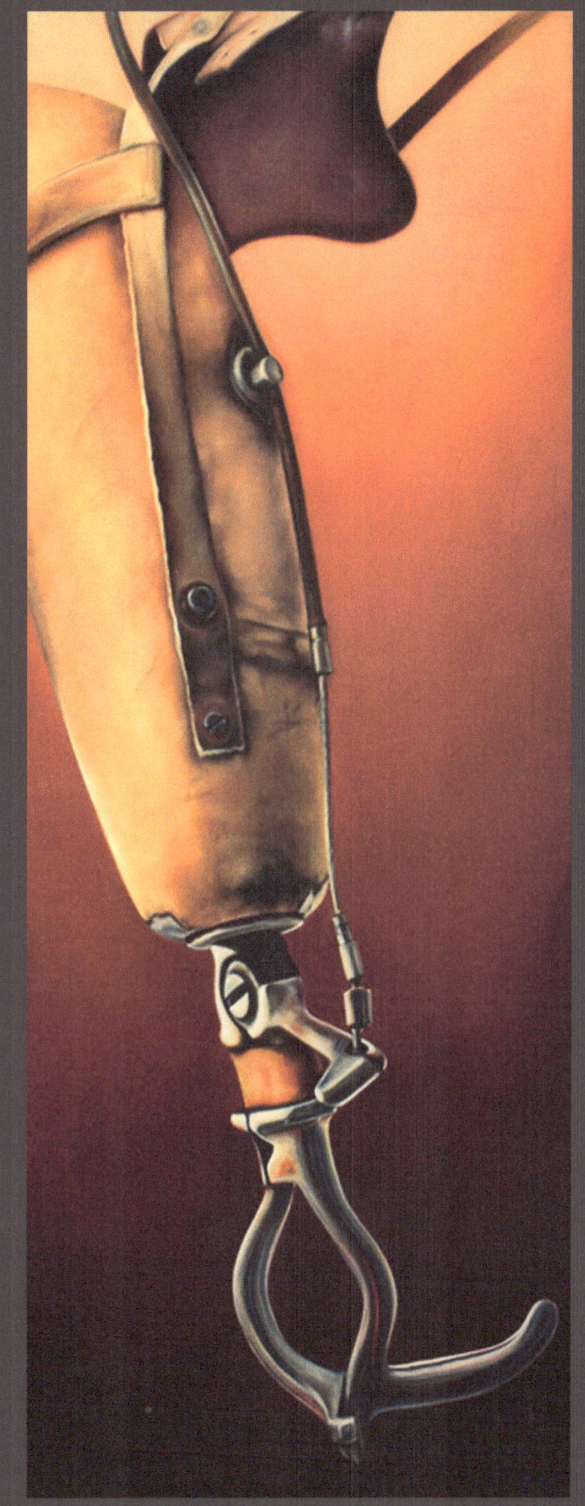

A Case of Living: Lee County, Exposure Study VI
**Oil on canvas
2'x1'6"**

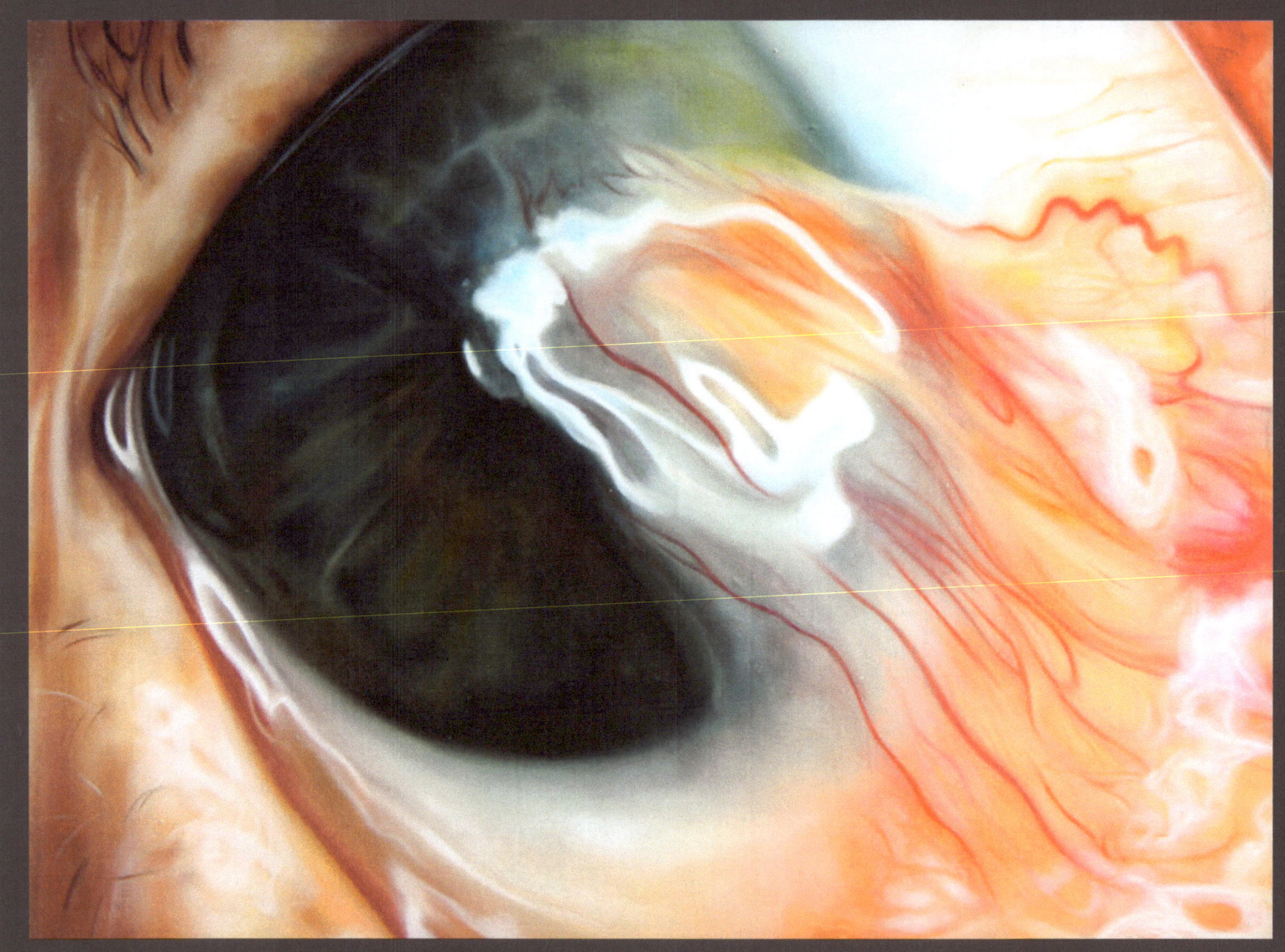

A Case of Living XIV: Fulton Co., Roots
Oil on canvas
2'5"x5'

Miranda Graham

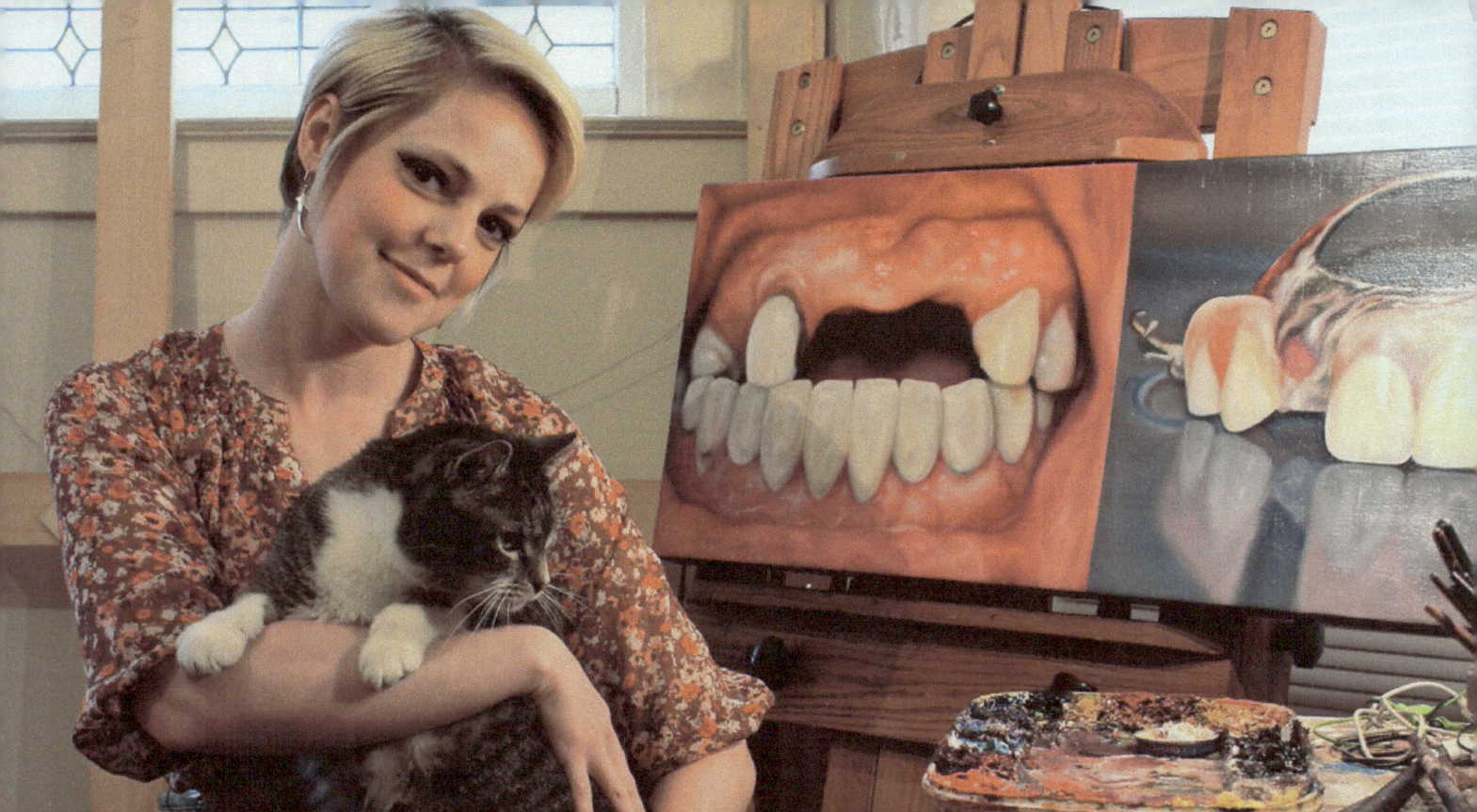

Miranda Graham, a native of Canton, Illinois, received her Bachelor's Degree in Fine Art from The School of the Art Institute in Chicago and her Master of Fine Arts under full scholarship, in painting, from Kendall College of Art & Design.

Graham is currently working as an adjunct professor with Ferris State University. Before attending Graduate school, Graham worked as a Program's Coordinator (Galleries Curator/Manager & Educator), for The Peoria Art Guild, in Peoria, IL for nearly four years. With a long career in public service & community collaborative art outreach, Graham specialized in expanding creative skill sets for the developmentally delayed and youth in crisis in the Chicago area.

Working primarily in oils, her paintings combine contemporary portraiture with vibrant color palettes to challenge formal assumptions about beauty. From small paintings of tooth decay to large scale, in-your-face hands, with missing fingers or distorted joints, these works bring a sense of dignity and heroic triumph to an otherwise discarded truth about our own humanity by examining physical imperfections with a passionate and personal encounter.

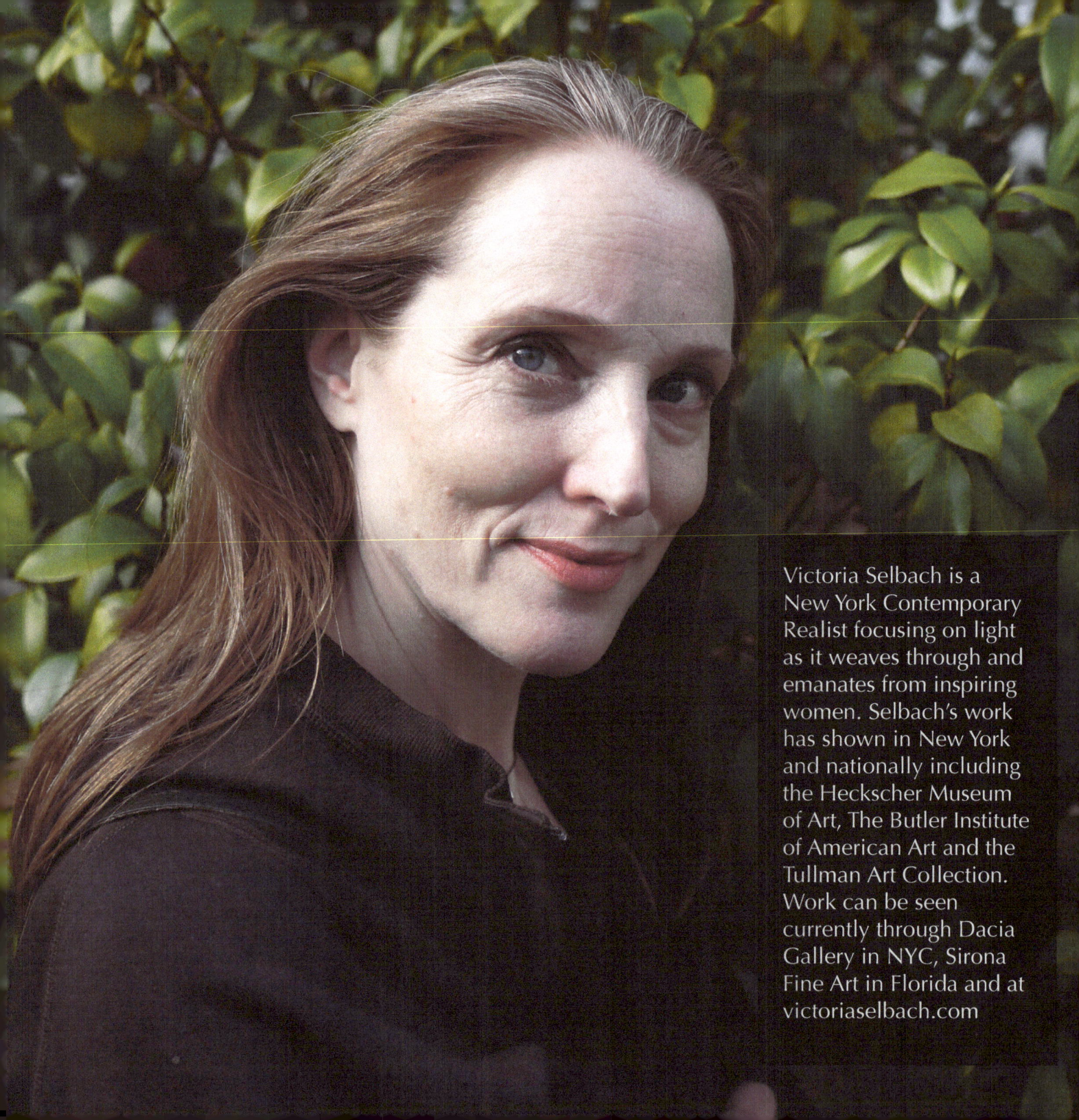

Victoria Selbach is a
New York Contemporary
Realist focusing on light
as it weaves through and
emanates from inspiring
women. Selbach's work
has shown in New York
and nationally including
the Heckscher Museum
of Art, The Butler Institute
of American Art and the
Tullman Art Collection.
Work can be seen
currently through Dacia
Gallery in NYC, Sirona
Fine Art in Florida and at
victoriaselbach.com

Victoria Selbach

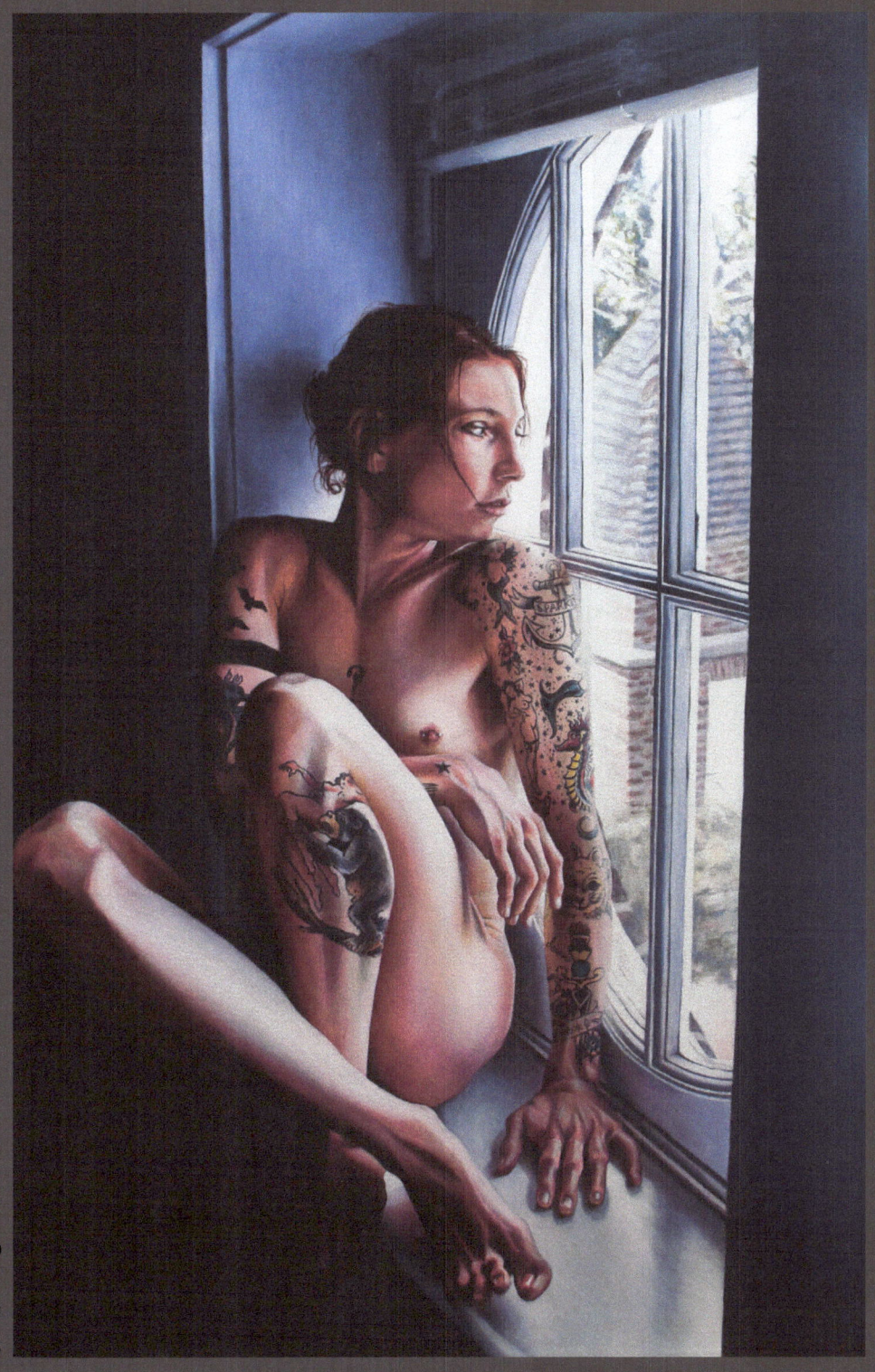

Dervish 2
Acrylic on canvas
46x30 inches

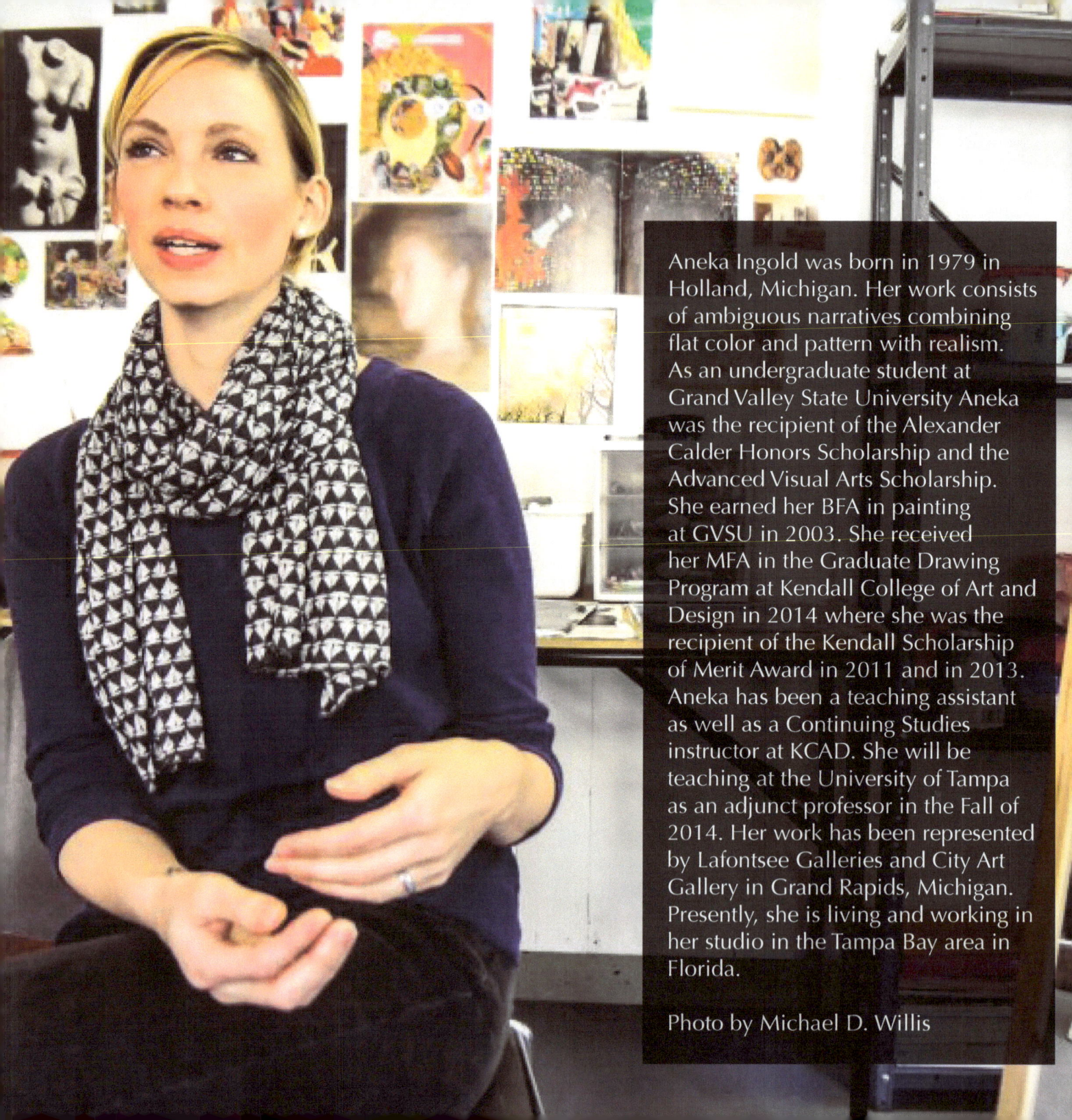

Aneka Ingold was born in 1979 in Holland, Michigan. Her work consists of ambiguous narratives combining flat color and pattern with realism. As an undergraduate student at Grand Valley State University Aneka was the recipient of the Alexander Calder Honors Scholarship and the Advanced Visual Arts Scholarship. She earned her BFA in painting at GVSU in 2003. She received her MFA in the Graduate Drawing Program at Kendall College of Art and Design in 2014 where she was the recipient of the Kendall Scholarship of Merit Award in 2011 and in 2013. Aneka has been a teaching assistant as well as a Continuing Studies instructor at KCAD. She will be teaching at the University of Tampa as an adjunct professor in the Fall of 2014. Her work has been represented by Lafontsee Galleries and City Art Gallery in Grand Rapids, Michigan. Presently, she is living and working in her studio in the Tampa Bay area in Florida.

Photo by Michael D. Willis

Aneka Ingold

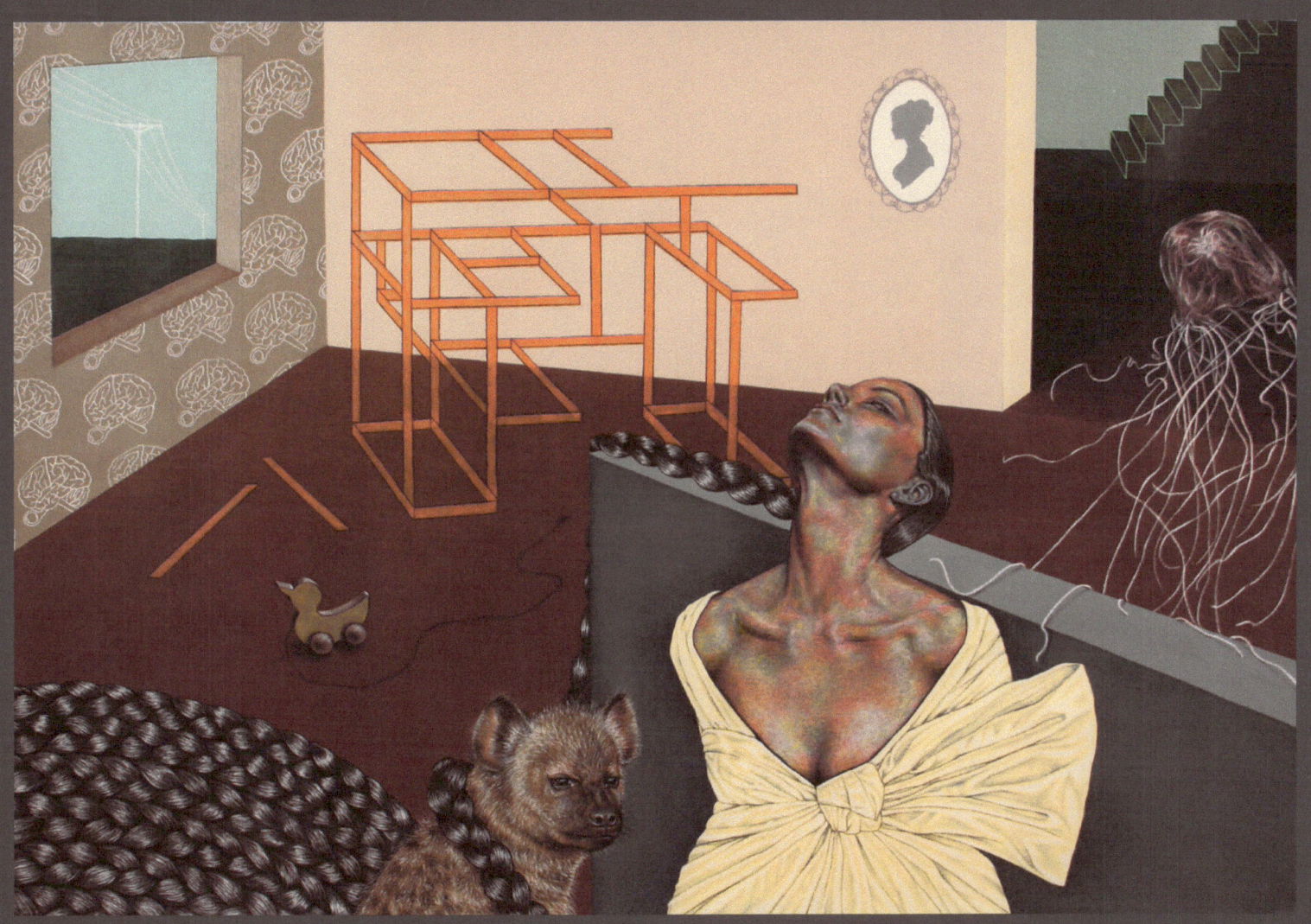

Blind Contemplation
Mixed media on paper
4x6 ft.

PA #55 Curated by Sergio Gomez May 2014

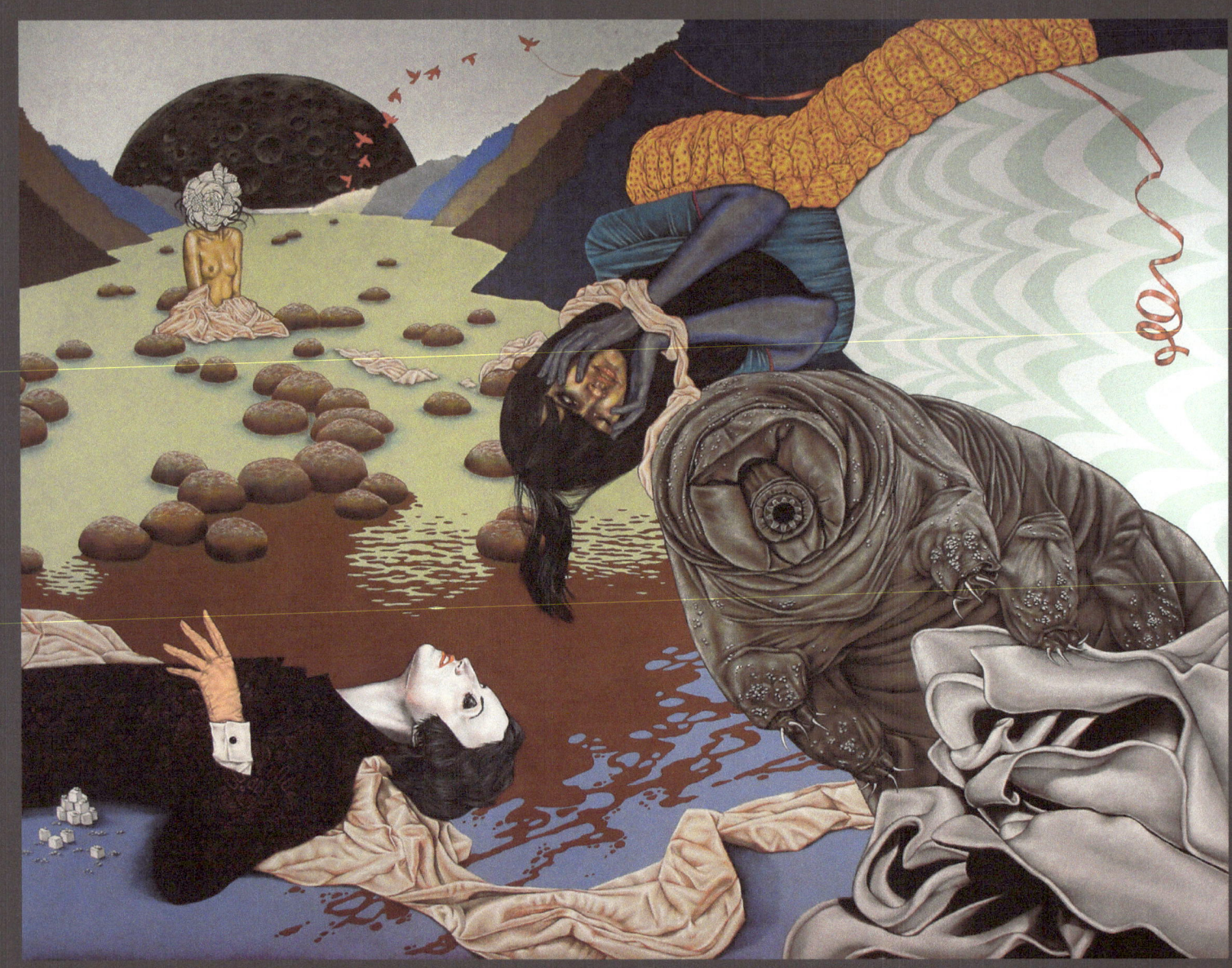

Insidious
Mixed media on vinyl
6x8 ft.

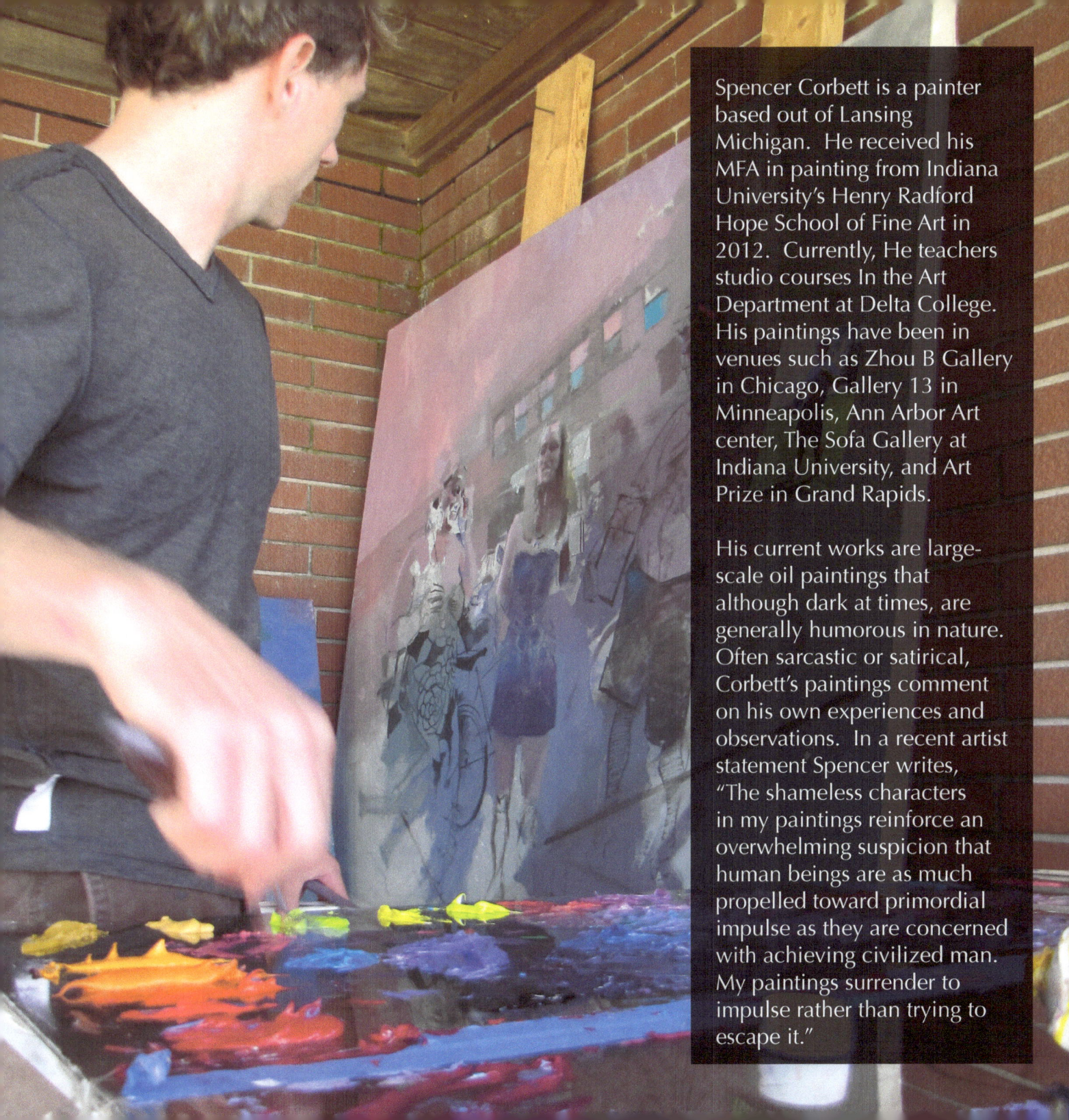

Spencer Corbett is a painter based out of Lansing Michigan. He received his MFA in painting from Indiana University's Henry Radford Hope School of Fine Art in 2012. Currently, He teachers studio courses In the Art Department at Delta College. His paintings have been in venues such as Zhou B Gallery in Chicago, Gallery 13 in Minneapolis, Ann Arbor Art center, The Sofa Gallery at Indiana University, and Art Prize in Grand Rapids.

His current works are large-scale oil paintings that although dark at times, are generally humorous in nature. Often sarcastic or satirical, Corbett's paintings comment on his own experiences and observations. In a recent artist statement Spencer writes, "The shameless characters in my paintings reinforce an overwhelming suspicion that human beings are as much propelled toward primordial impulse as they are concerned with achieving civilized man. My paintings surrender to impulse rather than trying to escape it."

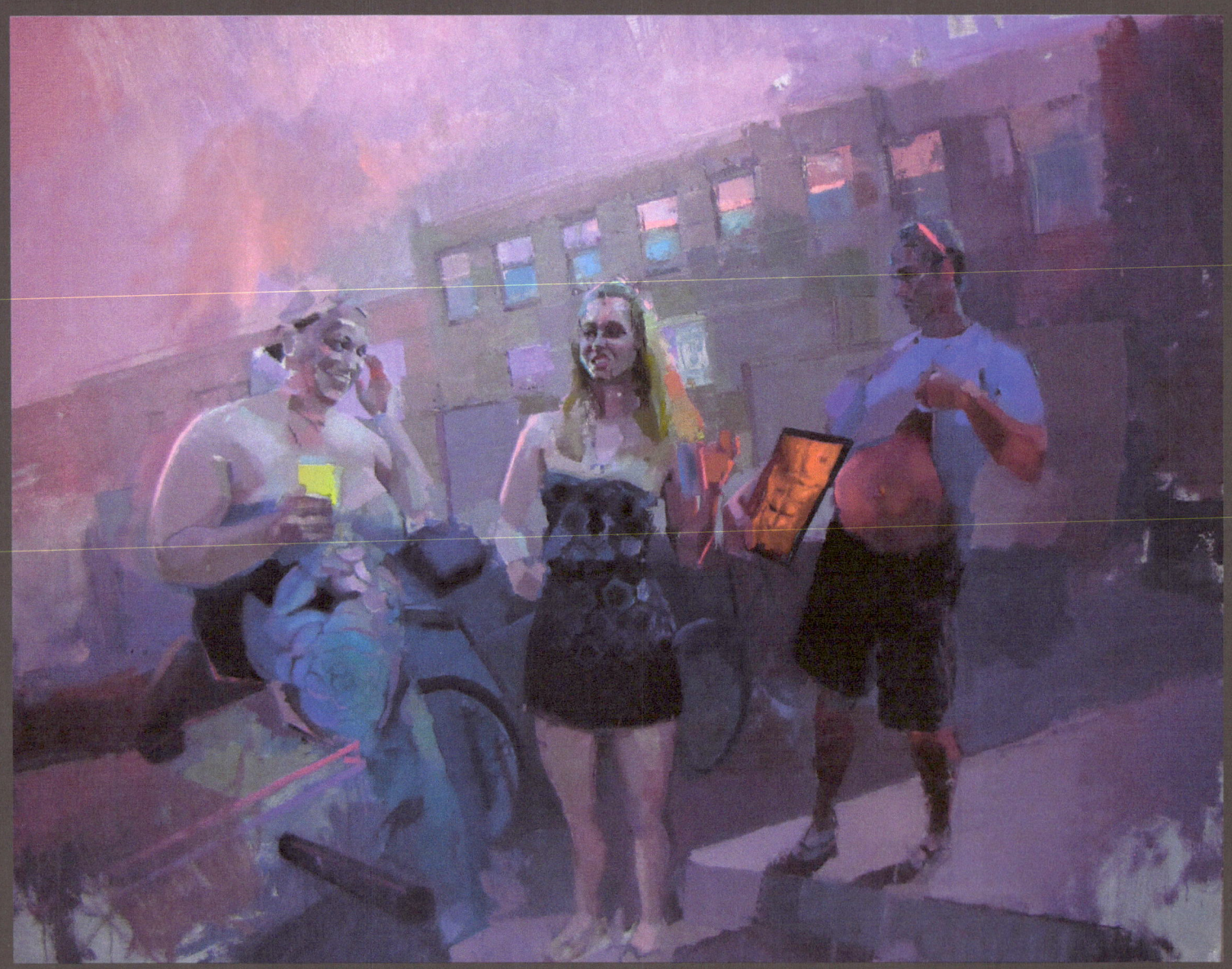

Flexin' Apps
Oil on canvas
48x60 inches

PA #55 Curated by Sergio Gomez May 2014

Cesar Santos

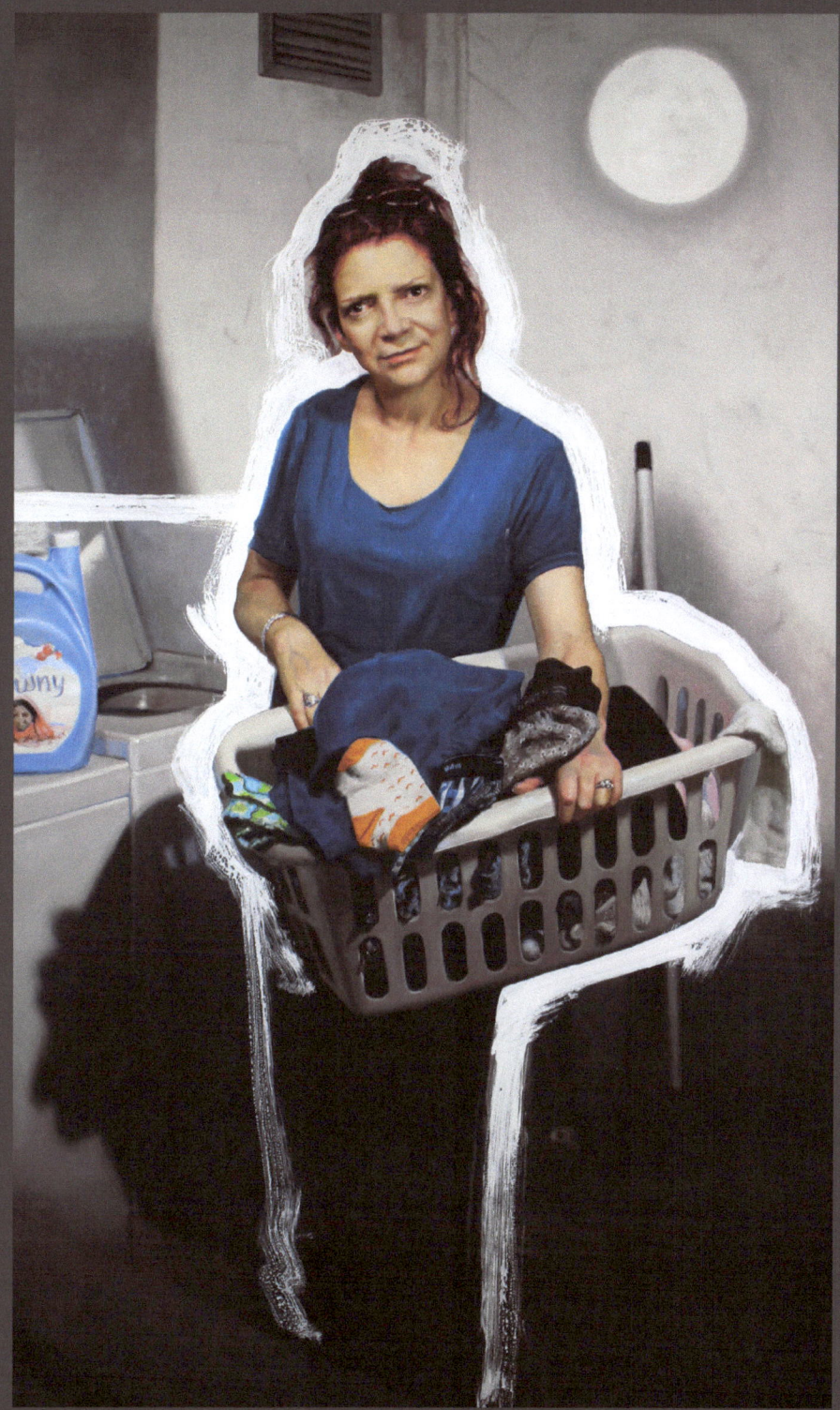

Siomara
Oil on linen
66x40 inches

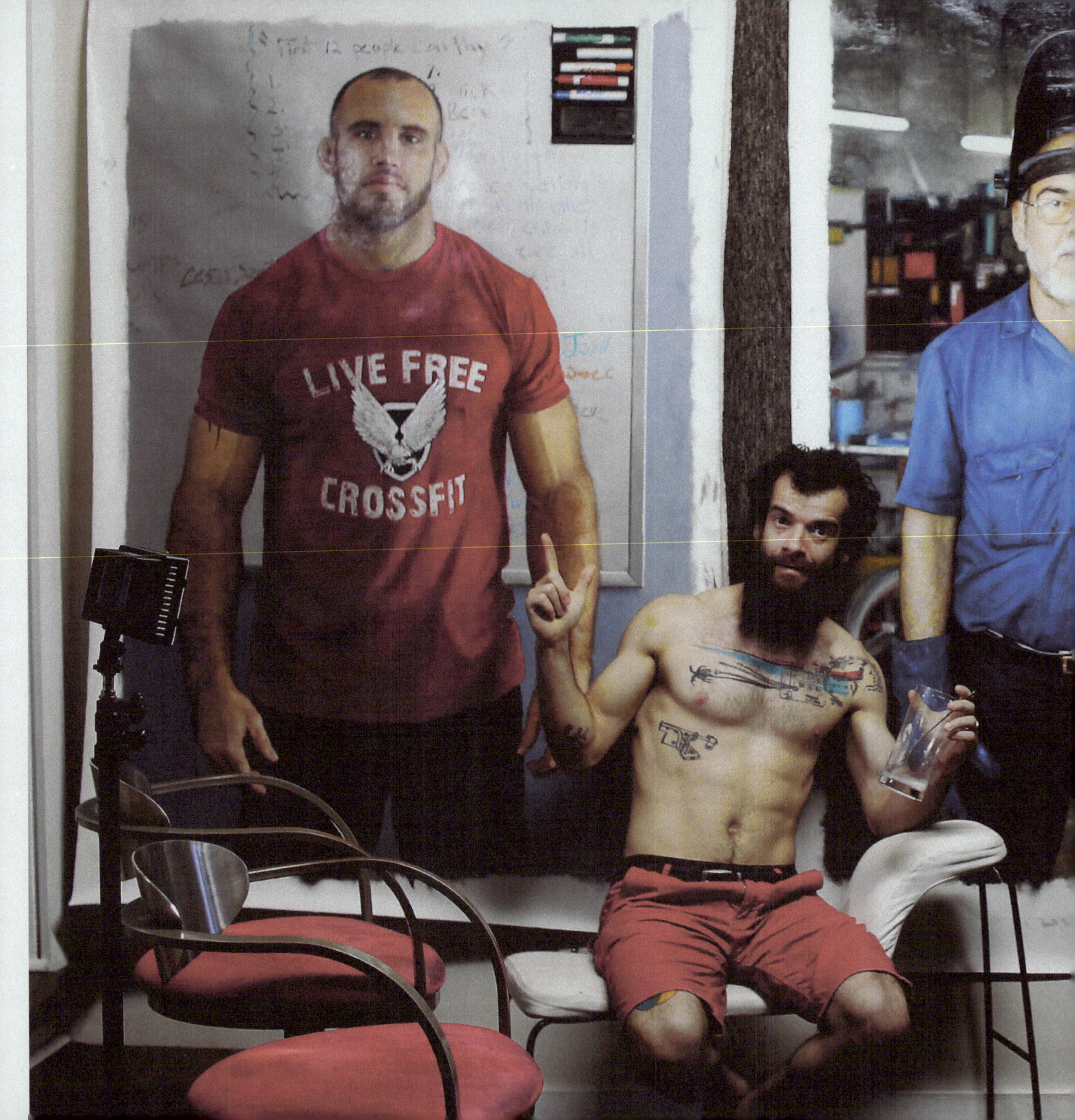

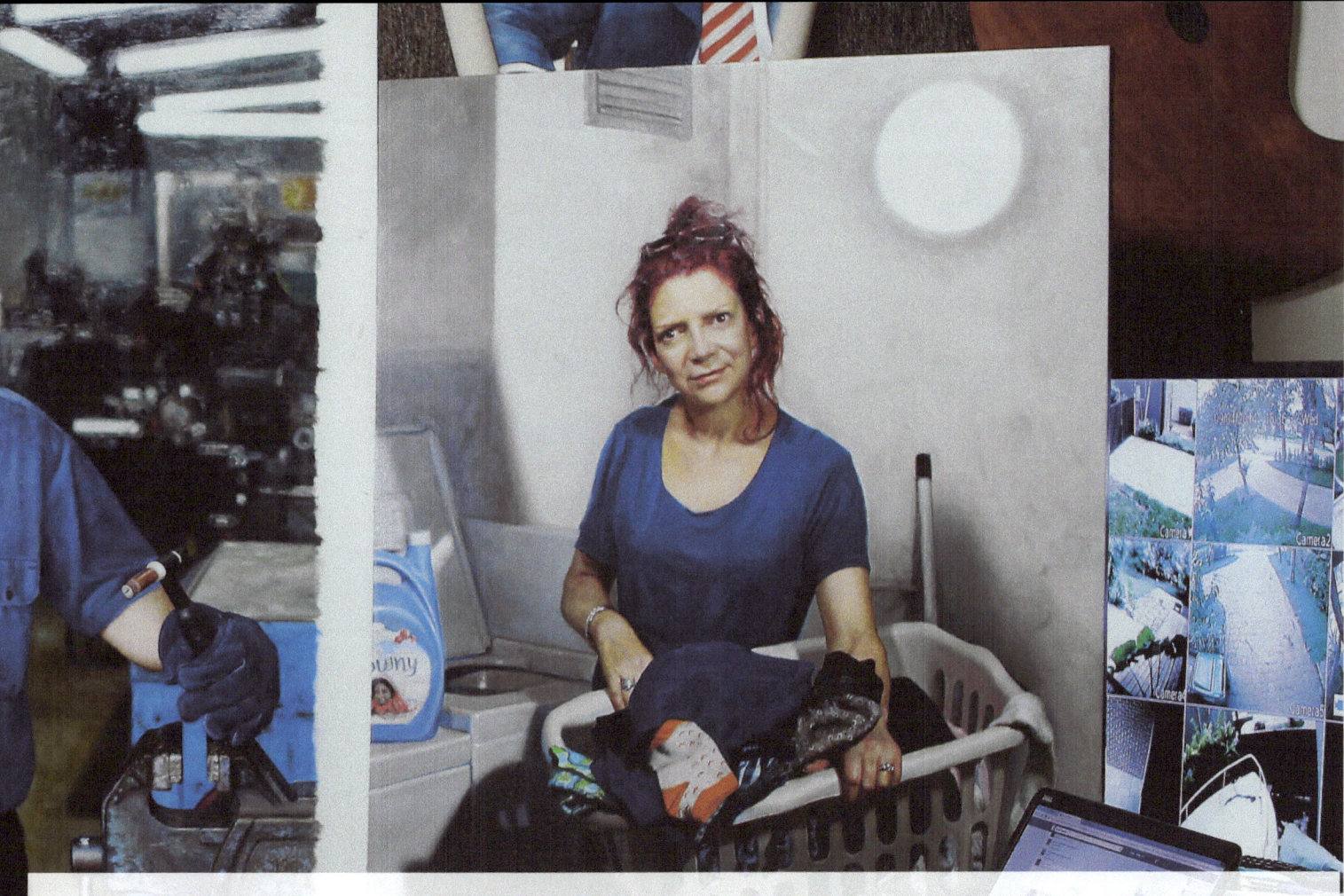

Cesar Santos (b. 1982), Cuban-American.
His art education is worldly, and his work has been seen around the globe, from the Annigoni Museum in Italy and the Beijing museum in China to Chelsea NY.

Santos studied at Miami Dade College, where he earned his associate in arts degree in 2003. He then attended the New World School of the Arts before traveling to Florence, Italy. In 2006, he completed the Angel Academy of Art in Florence studying under Michael John Angel, a student of artist Pietro Annigoni.

Santos' work reflects both classical and modern interpretations juxtaposed within one painting. His influences range from the Renaissance to the masters of the nineteenth century to Contemporary Art. With superb technique, he infuses a harmony between the natural and the conceptual to create works that are provocative and dramatic.

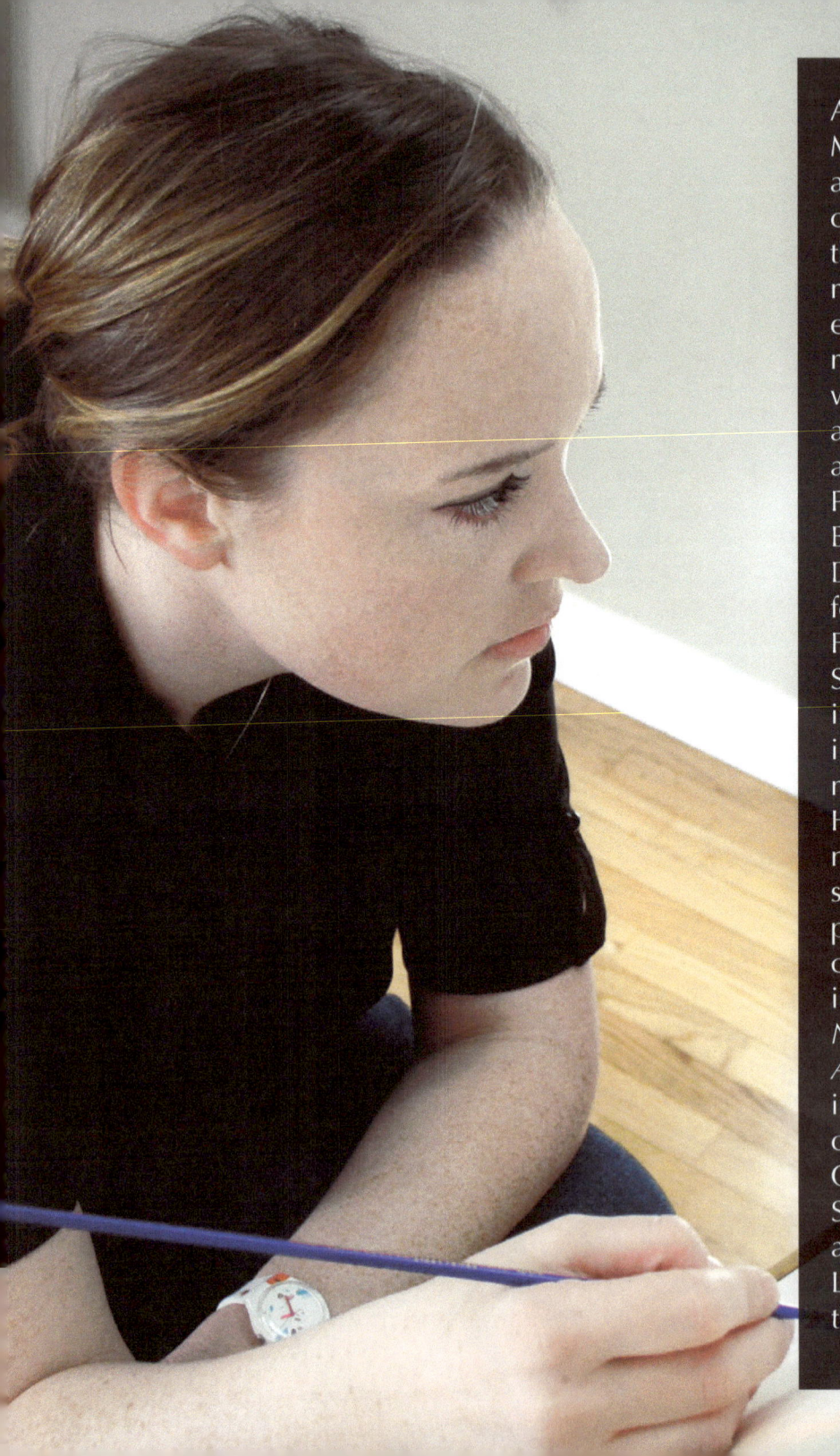

Ali Cavanaugh was born in St. Louis, Missouri in 1973 and has worked as a professional artist for 19 years. Her compositions are strong and intuitive, thanks not only to being a wife and mother but also to the variations in her experience—such as hearing loss—that made her adapt to and recreate the world around her. She studied painting at Kendall College of Art and Design and the New York Studio Residency Program in New York City, earning a BFA from Kendall College of Art and Design in 1995. In 1996, she co-founded the New School Academy of Fine Art in Grand Rapids, Michigan. She relocated to Santa Fe, New Mexico in 2000. It was during her seven years in Santa Fe that she developed her modern fresco process on kaolin clay. Her paintings have been the subject of numerous national and international solo and group exhibitions. Cavanaugh's paintings have been featured on book covers, countless internet features, and in many print publications including *The New York Times Magazine* and *American Artist Watercolor*. Her work is featured in more than 600 private and corporate collections throughout the United States, Canada, England, Germany, Portugal, Switzerland, Greece, France, Singapore, and Australia. She currently lives in St Louis, Missouri with her husband and their four children.

Ali Cavanaugh

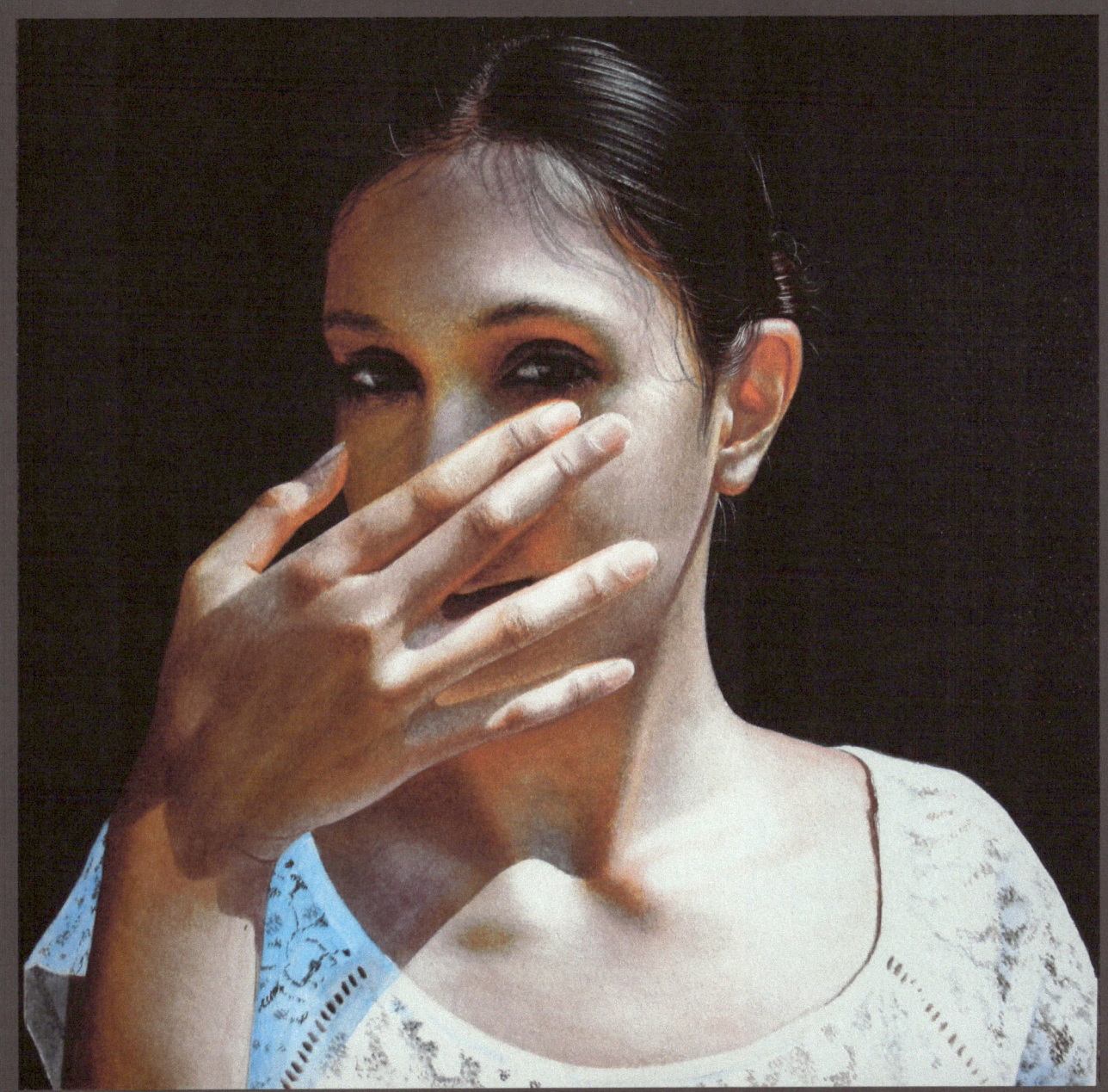

to remember what I saw
Modern Fresco
8x8 inches

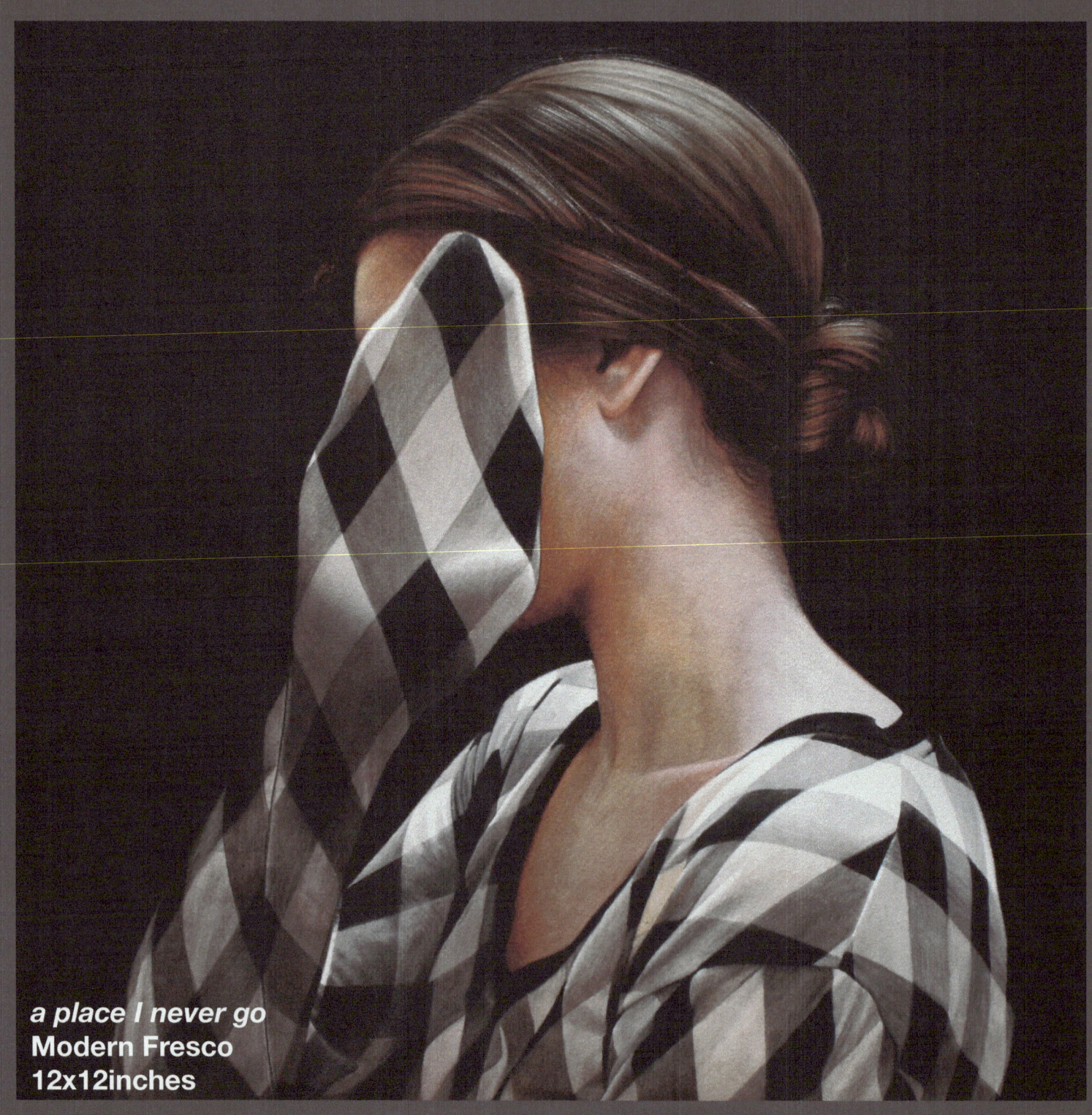

a place I never go
Modern Fresco
12x12inches

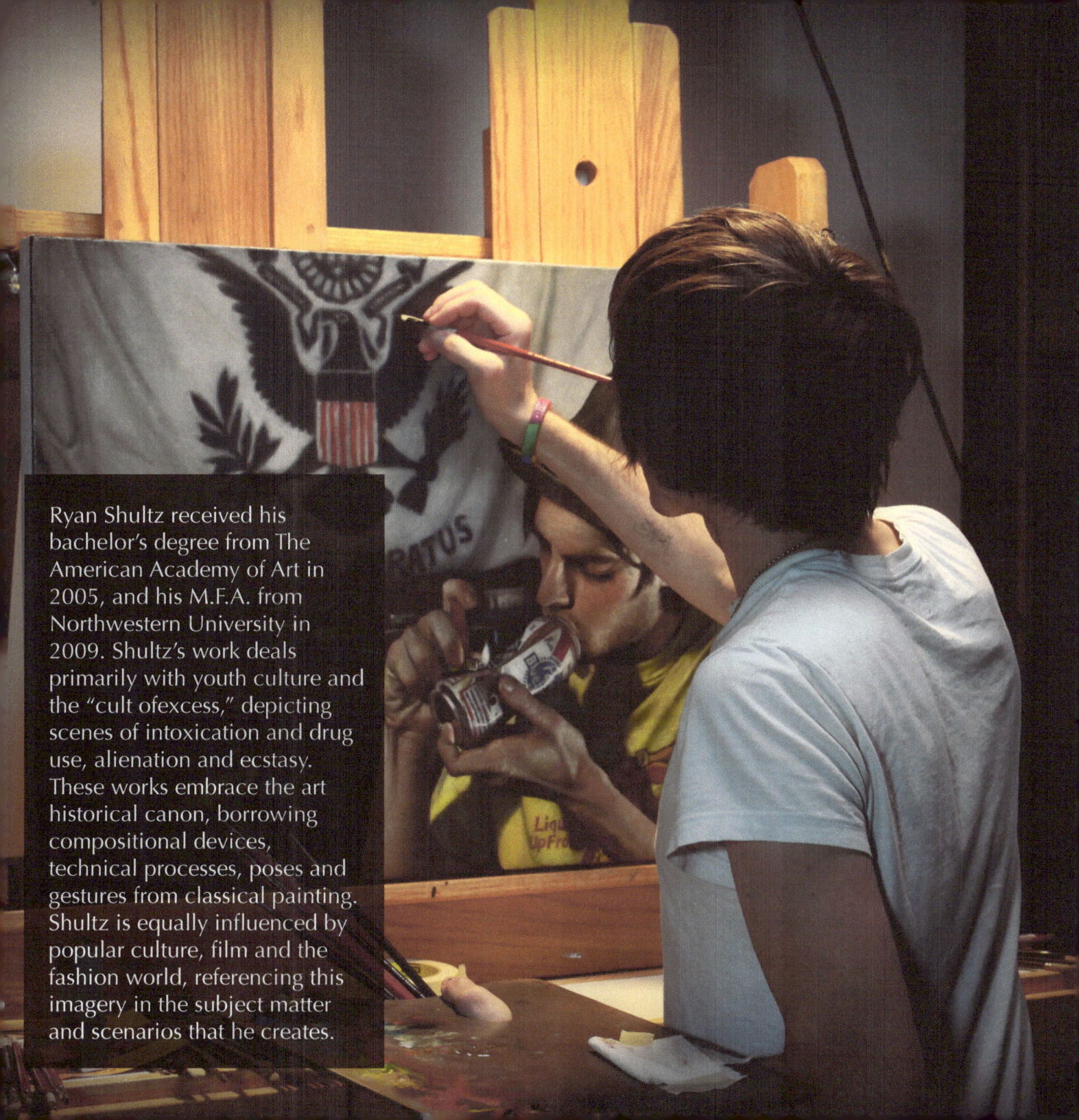

Ryan Shultz received his bachelor's degree from The American Academy of Art in 2005, and his M.F.A. from Northwestern University in 2009. Shultz's work deals primarily with youth culture and the "cult ofexcess," depicting scenes of intoxication and drug use, alienation and ecstasy. These works embrace the art historical canon, borrowing compositional devices, technical processes, poses and gestures from classical painting. Shultz is equally influenced by popular culture, film and the fashion world, referencing this imagery in the subject matter and scenarios that he creates.

Ryan Shultz

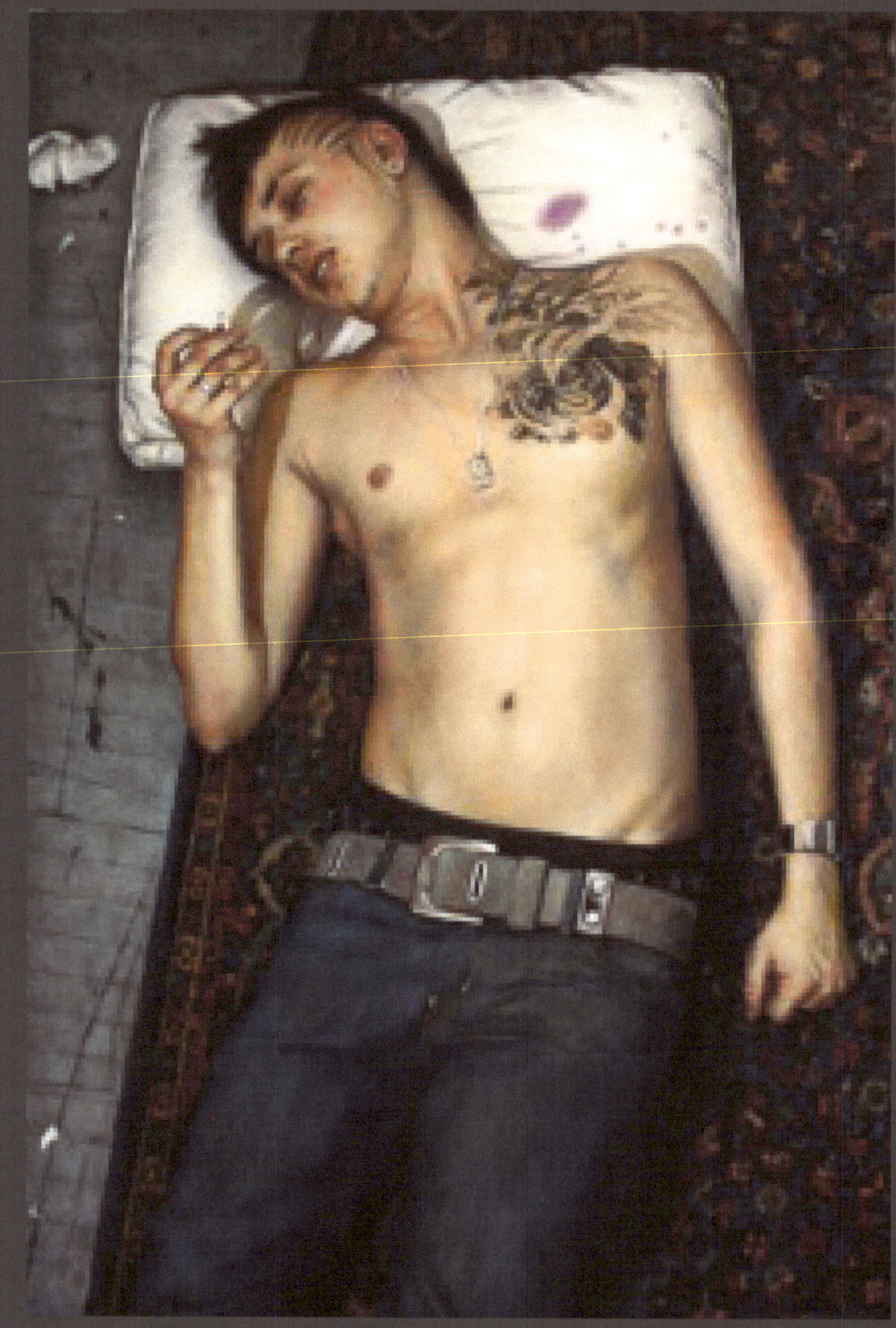

Jakub Smoking
Oil on linen
48 x 32 inches

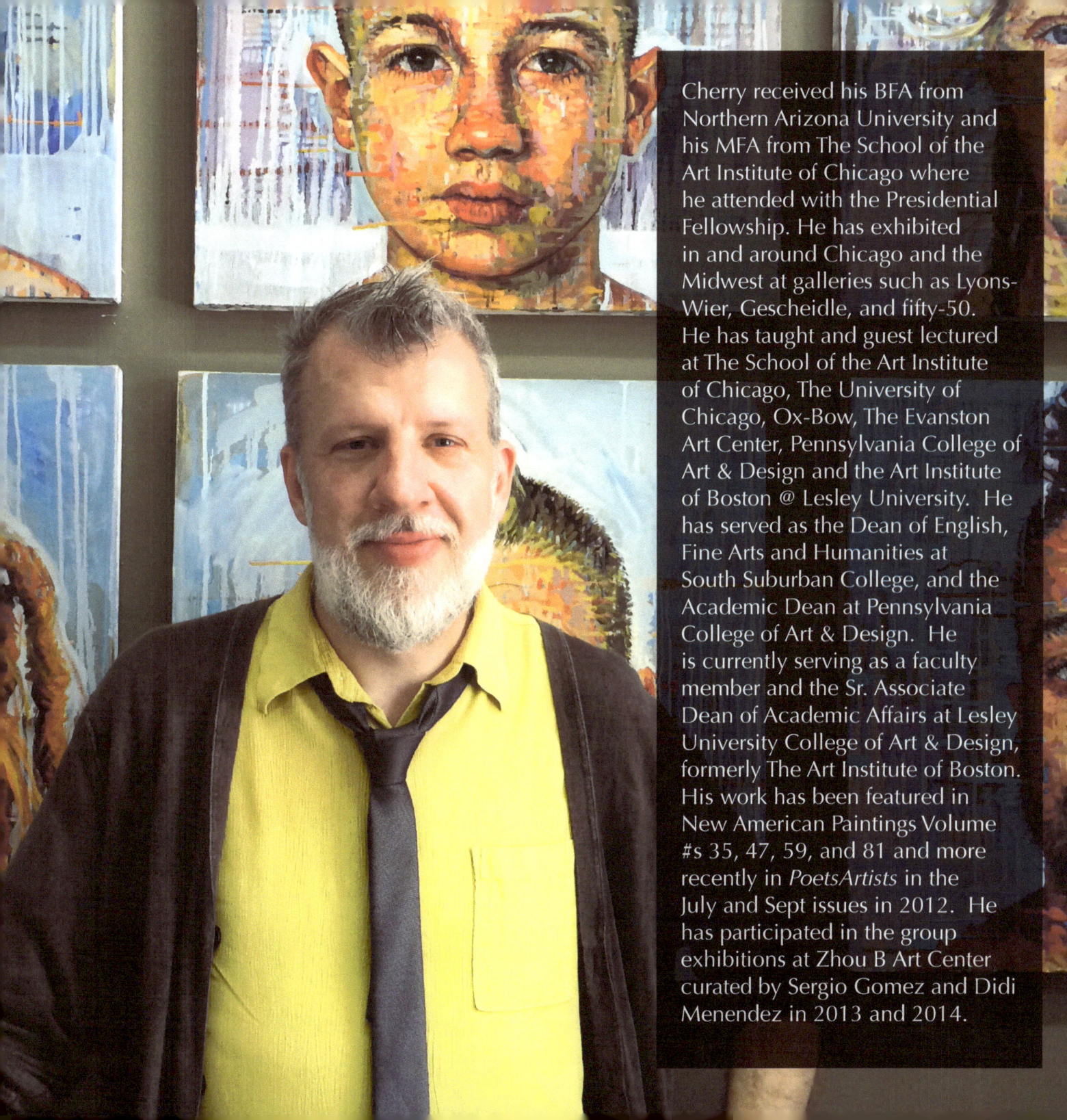

Cherry received his BFA from Northern Arizona University and his MFA from The School of the Art Institute of Chicago where he attended with the Presidential Fellowship. He has exhibited in and around Chicago and the Midwest at galleries such as Lyons-Wier, Gescheidle, and fifty-50. He has taught and guest lectured at The School of the Art Institute of Chicago, The University of Chicago, Ox-Bow, The Evanston Art Center, Pennsylvania College of Art & Design and the Art Institute of Boston @ Lesley University. He has served as the Dean of English, Fine Arts and Humanities at South Suburban College, and the Academic Dean at Pennsylvania College of Art & Design. He is currently serving as a faculty member and the Sr. Associate Dean of Academic Affairs at Lesley University College of Art & Design, formerly The Art Institute of Boston. His work has been featured in New American Paintings Volume #s 35, 47, 59, and 81 and more recently in *PoetsArtists* in the July and Sept issues in 2012. He has participated in the group exhibitions at Zhou B Art Center curated by Sergio Gomez and Didi Menendez in 2013 and 2014.

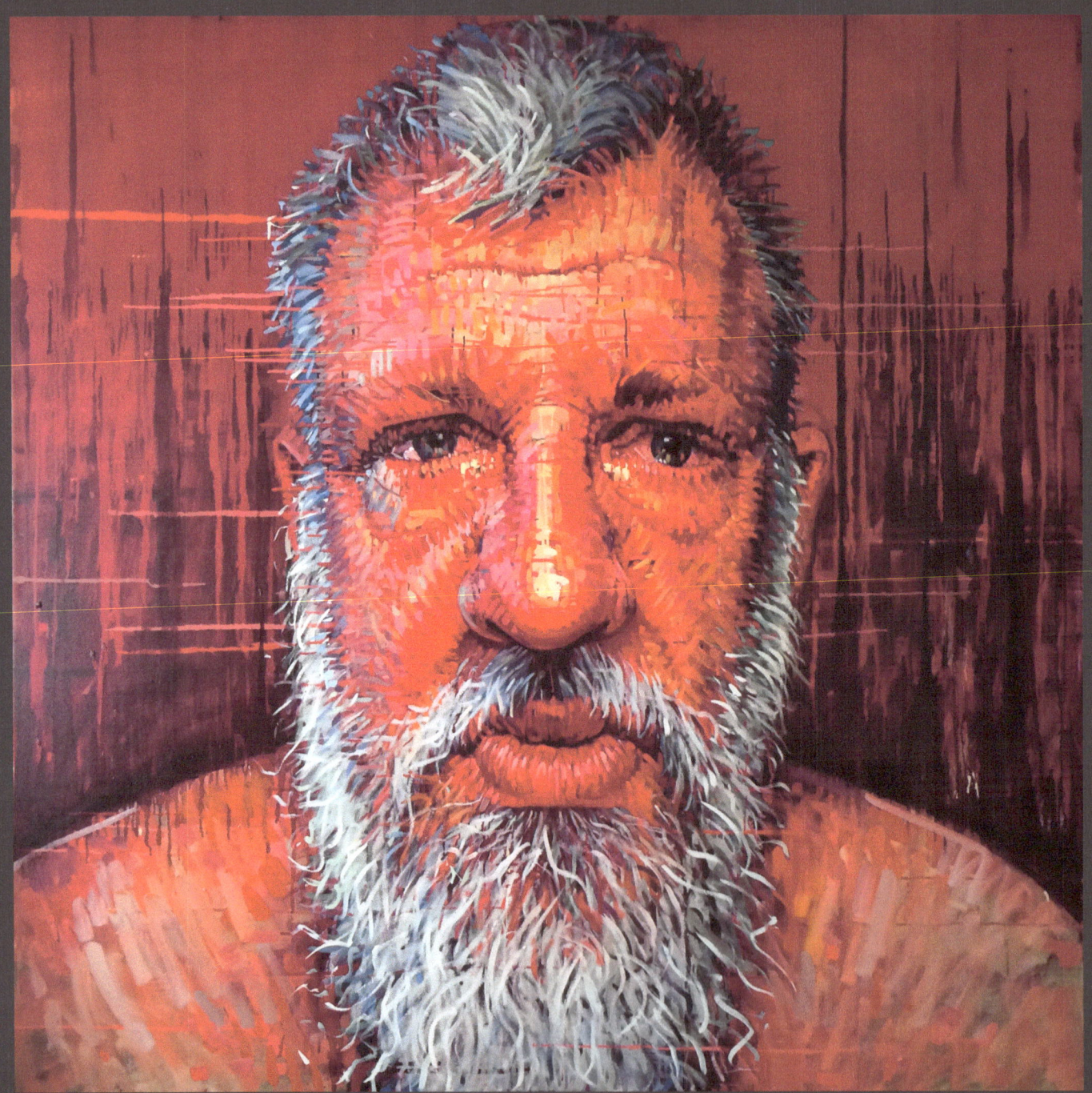

Mad Red Face
Oil on canvas
68x68 inches

Matthew Cherry

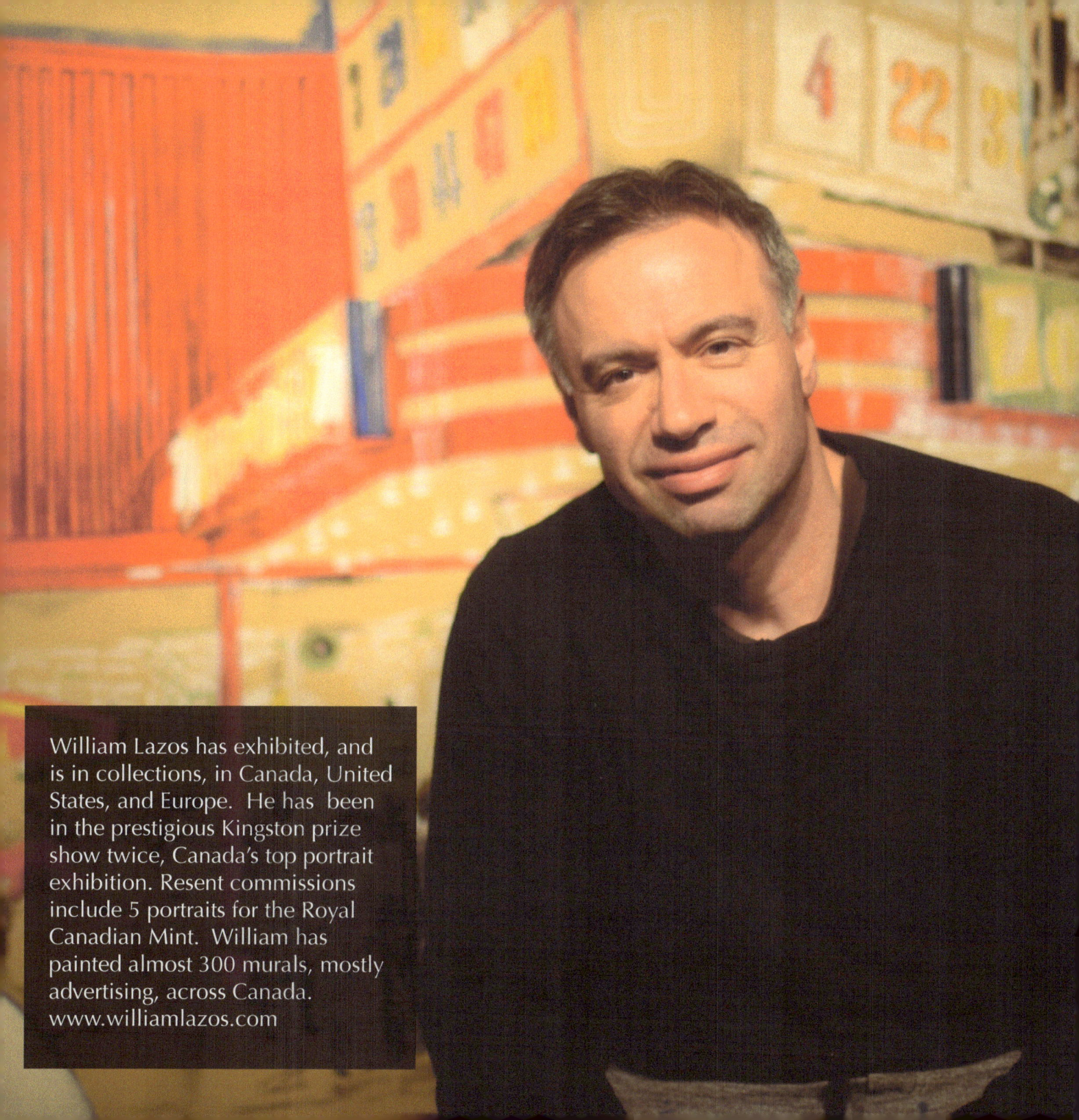

William Lazos has exhibited, and is in collections, in Canada, United States, and Europe. He has been in the prestigious Kingston prize show twice, Canada's top portrait exhibition. Resent commissions include 5 portraits for the Royal Canadian Mint. William has painted almost 300 murals, mostly advertising, across Canada.
www.williamlazos.com

William Lazos

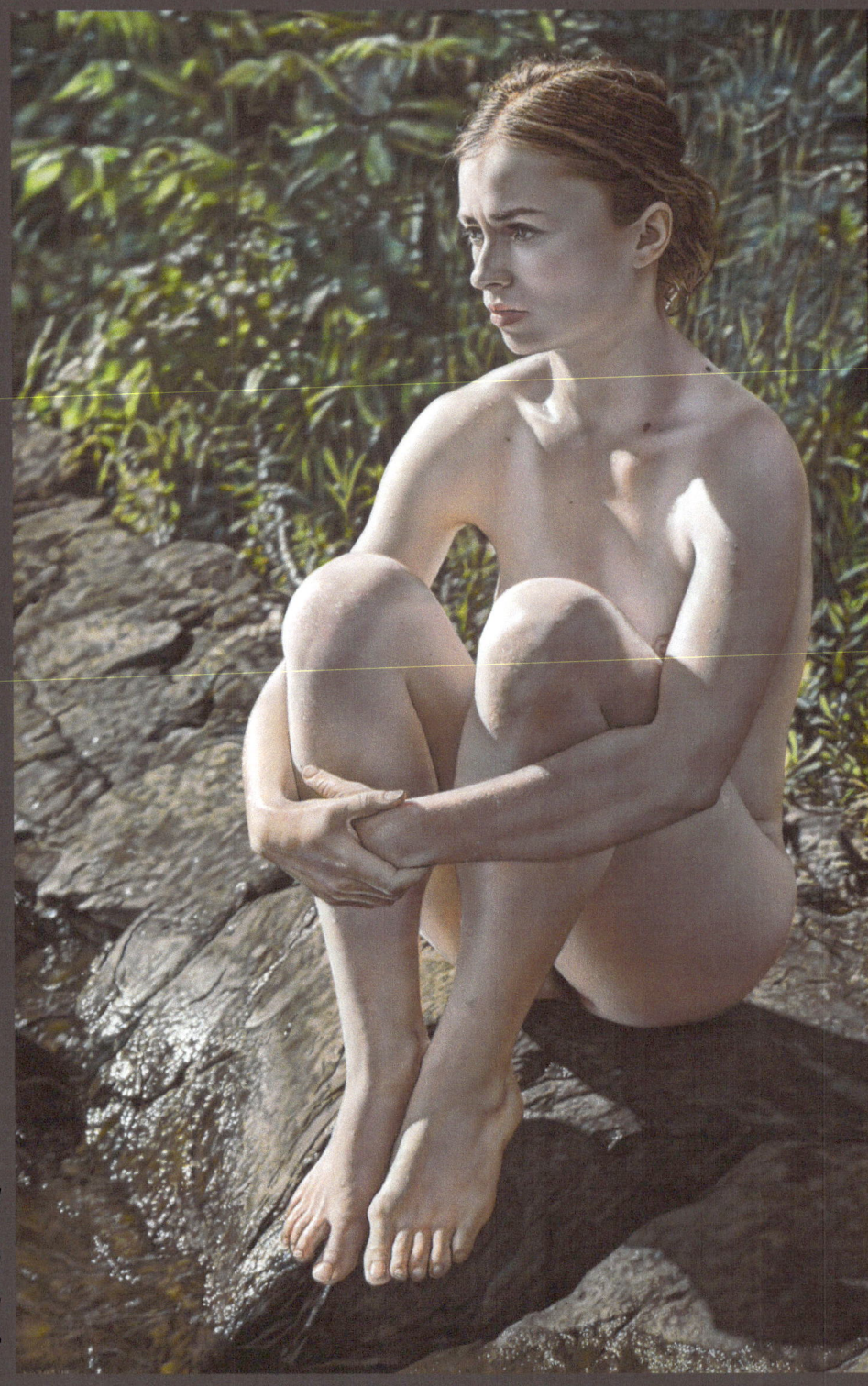

Penny VII
Acrylic on canvas
30 x 48 inches
2014

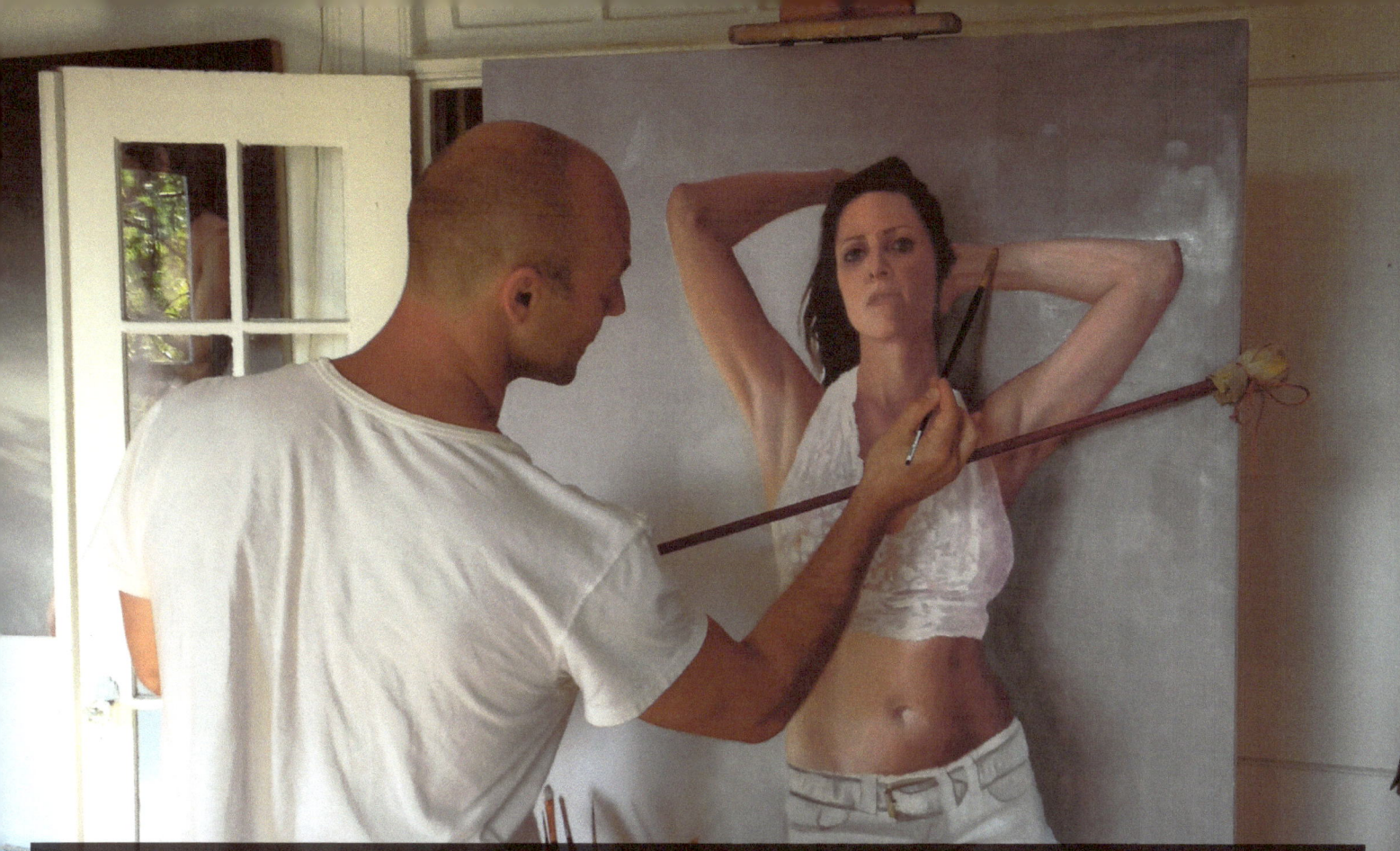

Aleksander Betko is an artist whose contemporary appeal is firmly—and poignantly—rooted in the New York City of decades past. Born in Poland in 1976, his family fled the political unrest in that country when he was four years old, settling in Queens. Betko subsequently spent his youth immersed in the city's dynamic culture, both established (museums, art mentors) and underground (the 1980s punk scene, street performers). Those influences constantly linger in his work today.

But it wasn't until he finished art school at SUNY Purchase at the age of 20 that Betko made his way to Brooklyn, and "was in love right from the start," as he puts it. It was here that he developed his artistic polish, producing works that evoke moments of solitude and otherness within the kinetic rumble of New York. His most recent show, at the Dacia Gallery last summer, presented a series of intimate portraits of creative New Yorkers caught in various moments of contemplation and brought a good amount of well deserved attention to his work.

aleksanderbetko.com

Aleksander Betko

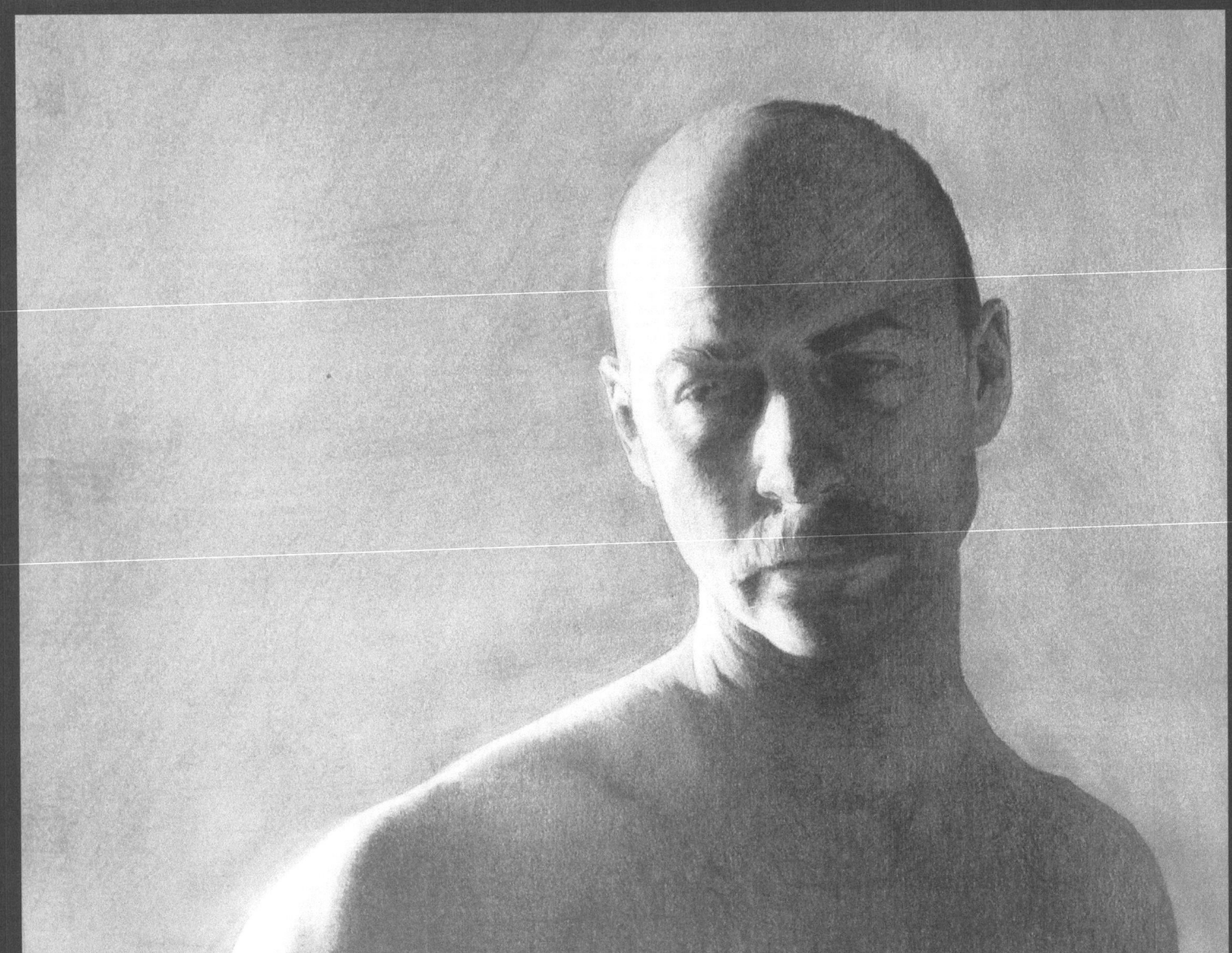

Leviathan
Graphite Pencil on Stonehedge Warm White Printing Paper
12.5x15.5 inches

PA #55 Curated by Sergio Gomez May 2014

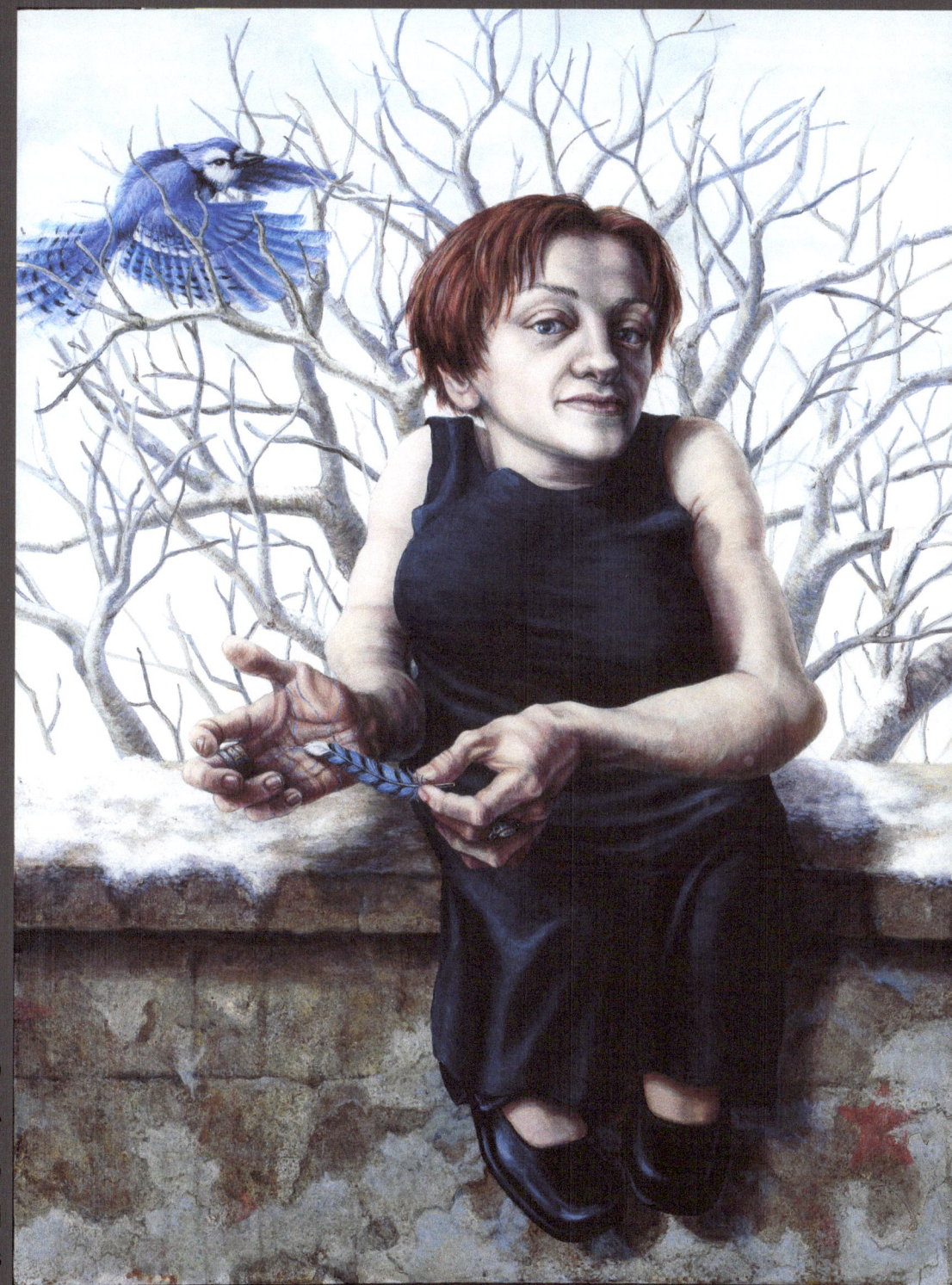

Riva Lehrer

Rebecca
Maskos
(Circle Stories)
Acrylic on panel
24 x 18 inches

Riva Lehrer (b. Cincinnati 1958) has exhibited in museums and galleries across the country. Her work focuses on issues of physical identity and the socially challenged body.

Ms. Lehrer's work has been seen in venues including the United Nations, the National Museum of Women in the Arts in Washington, DC, the Arnot Museum, the DeCordova Museum, the Frye Museum, the Smithsonian Museum, the Chicago Cultural Center, the State of Illinois Museum, and the Elmhurst Museum. She has been a visiting artist and lecturer across the US and Europe.

Her work with graphic novelist Alison Bechdel is the subject of a 2012 documentary, "The Paper Mirror", by Charissa King-O'Brien, and is currently being shown in film festivals around the world. A 2005 documentary "Self Preservation: The Art of Riva Lehrer" by David Mitchell and Sharon Snyder has been seen at numerous film fests, winning awards and becoming included in many university curricula. She is also in 2 upcoming documentaries; "Variations" by Laurie Little and Anuradha Rana; and "Code of the Freaks" by Salome Chasnoff, Carrie Sandahl, and Susan Nussbaum.

Awards include the 2009 Prairie Fellowship at the Ragdale Foundation and 2009 the Critical Fierceness Grant, the 2008 Three Arts Foundation of Chicago grant for artistic achievement, and the 2006 Wynn Newhouse Award for Excellence, based in New York City, an unrestricted grant for $50,000. Other awards include those from the Illinois Arts Council, the University of Illinois and the National Endowment for the Arts.

Ms. Lehrer's writing and visual art are included in the new anthology, "Sex and Disability", Duke University Press, edited by Robert McRuer and Anna Mollow, 2011.

Riva Lehrer is currently adjunct professor at the School of the Art Institute of Chicago (Drawing and Anatomy), visiting artist in Medical Humanities at Northwestern University, and co-chair of the Chicago Bodies of Work Festival 2013.

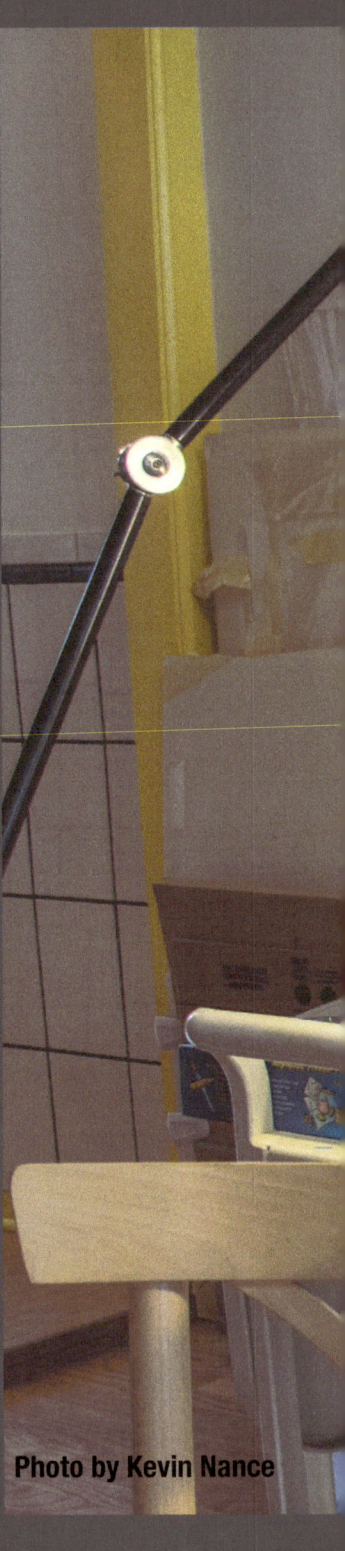

Photo by Kevin Nance

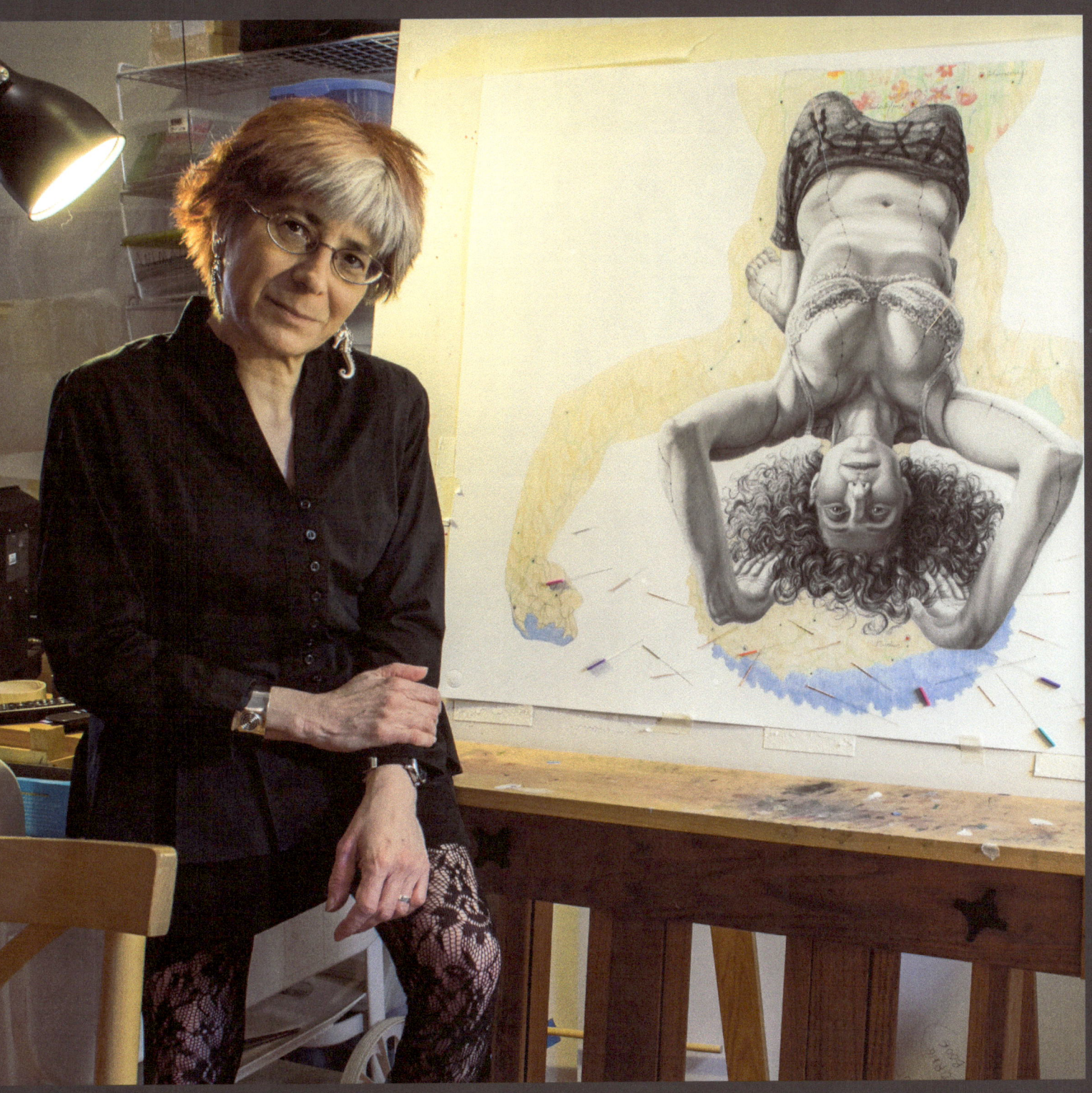

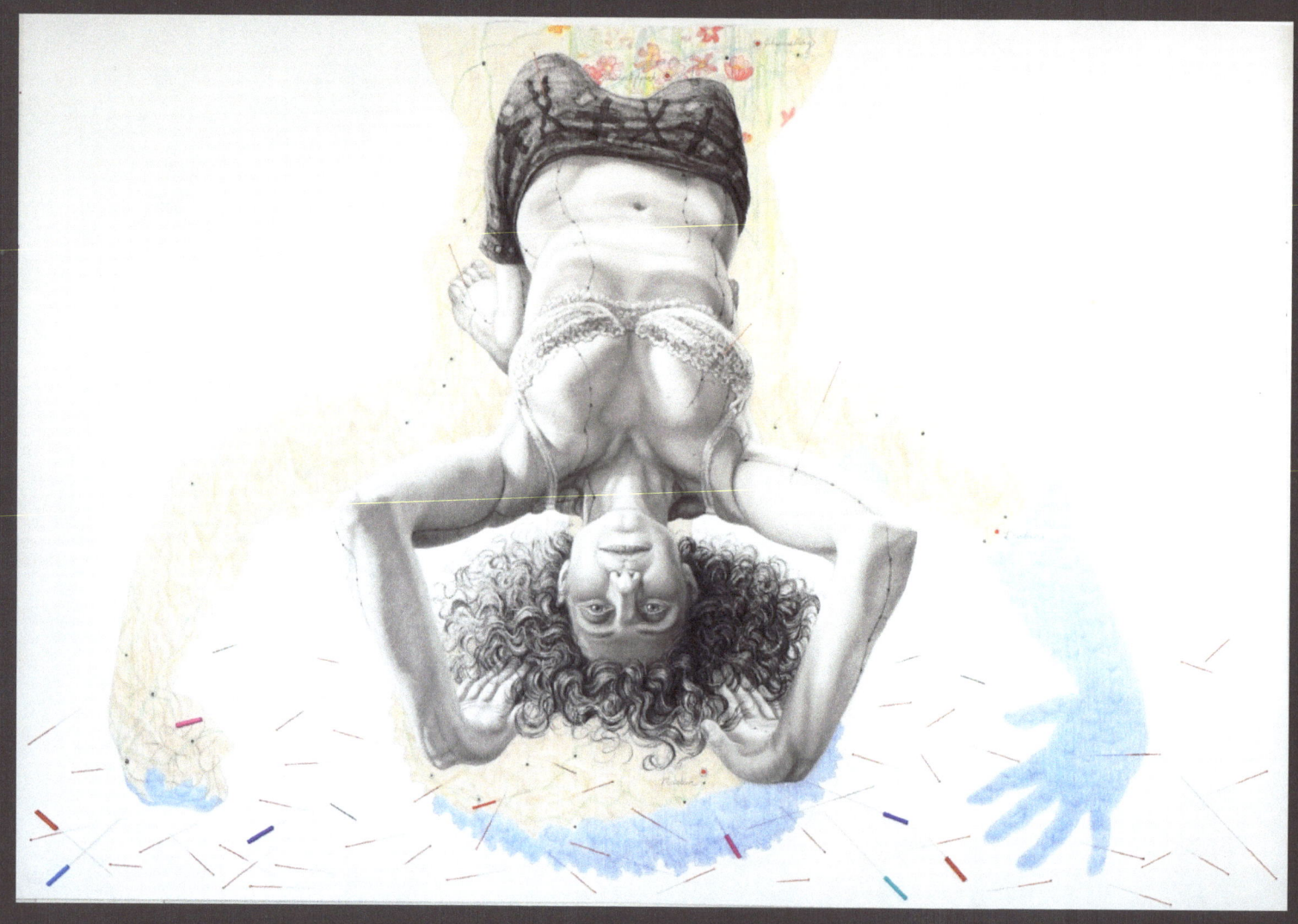

SUSPENSION: RR (Ghost Parade. Rhoda Rosen)
Charcoal, mixed media and
dimensional collage on paper
28 x 40 inches

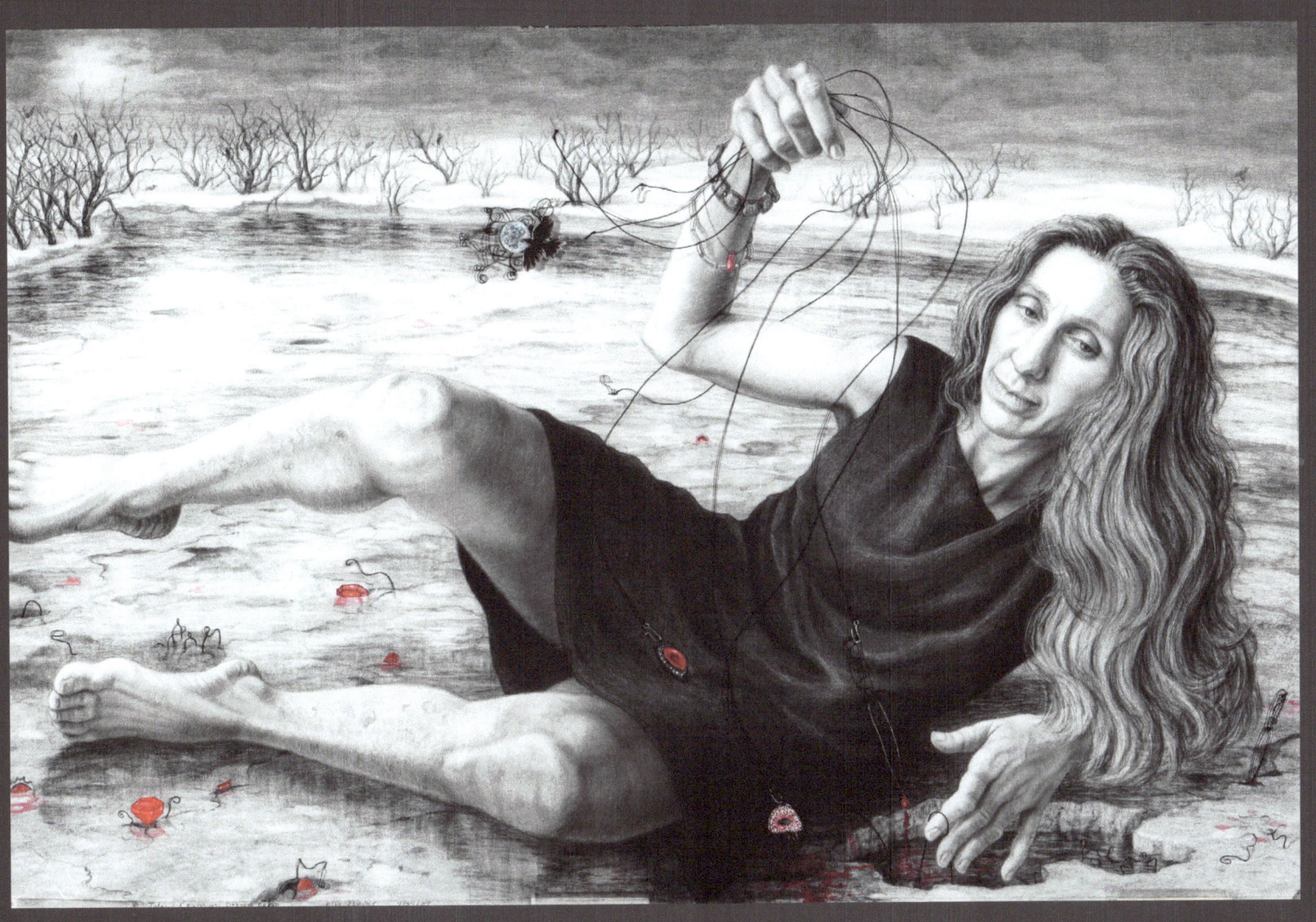

Deborah Brod (Totems and Familiars)
Charcoal, mixed media and
dimensional collage on paper
30 x 44 inches

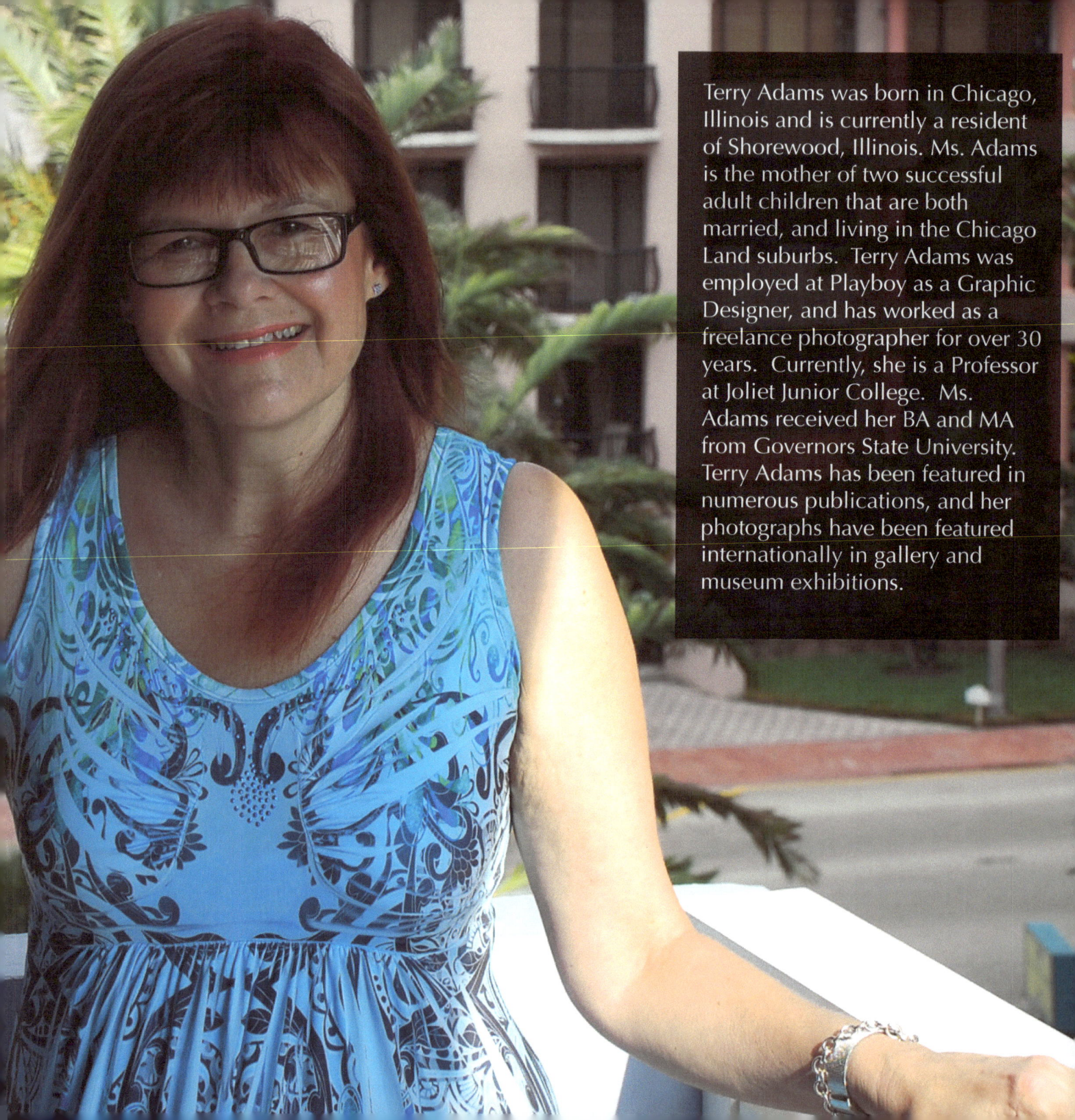

Terry Adams was born in Chicago, Illinois and is currently a resident of Shorewood, Illinois. Ms. Adams is the mother of two successful adult children that are both married, and living in the Chicago Land suburbs. Terry Adams was employed at Playboy as a Graphic Designer, and has worked as a freelance photographer for over 30 years. Currently, she is a Professor at Joliet Junior College. Ms. Adams received her BA and MA from Governors State University. Terry Adams has been featured in numerous publications, and her photographs have been featured internationally in gallery and museum exhibitions.

Terry Adams

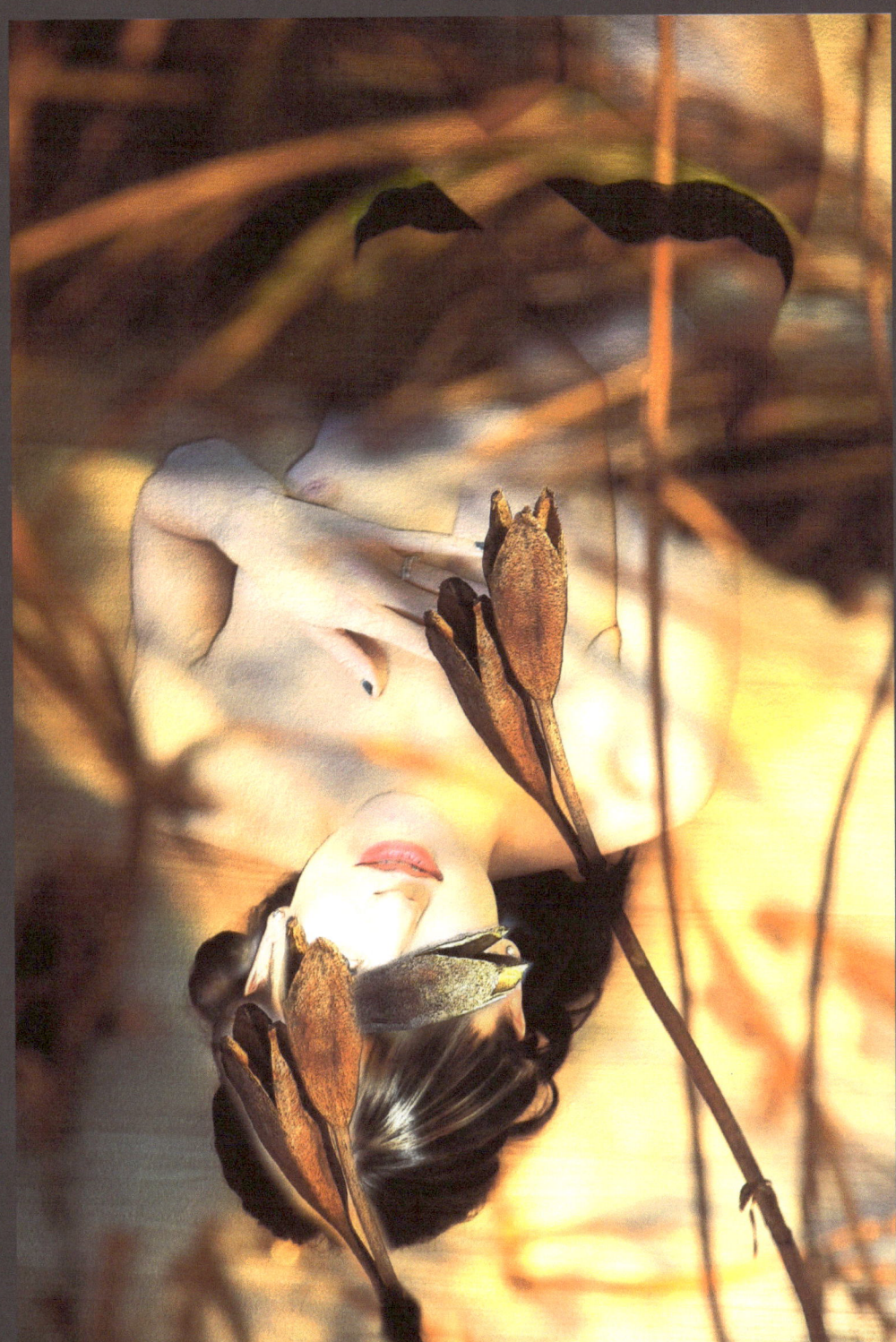

One with the Earth
Montage Collage
16 x 24 inches

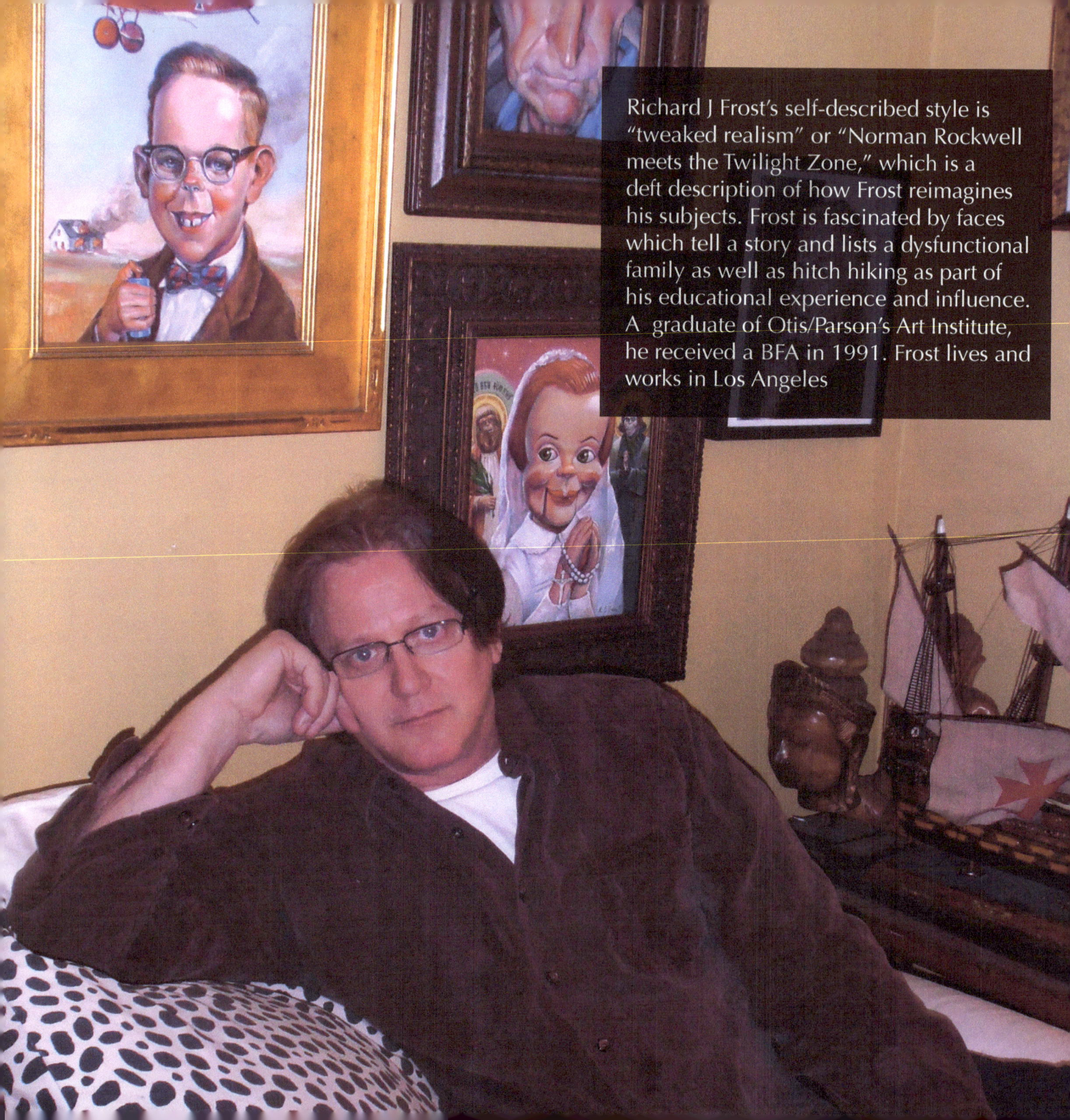

Richard J Frost's self-described style is "tweaked realism" or "Norman Rockwell meets the Twilight Zone," which is a deft description of how Frost reimagines his subjects. Frost is fascinated by faces which tell a story and lists a dysfunctional family as well as hitch hiking as part of his educational experience and influence. A graduate of Otis/Parson's Art Institute, he received a BFA in 1991. Frost lives and works in Los Angeles

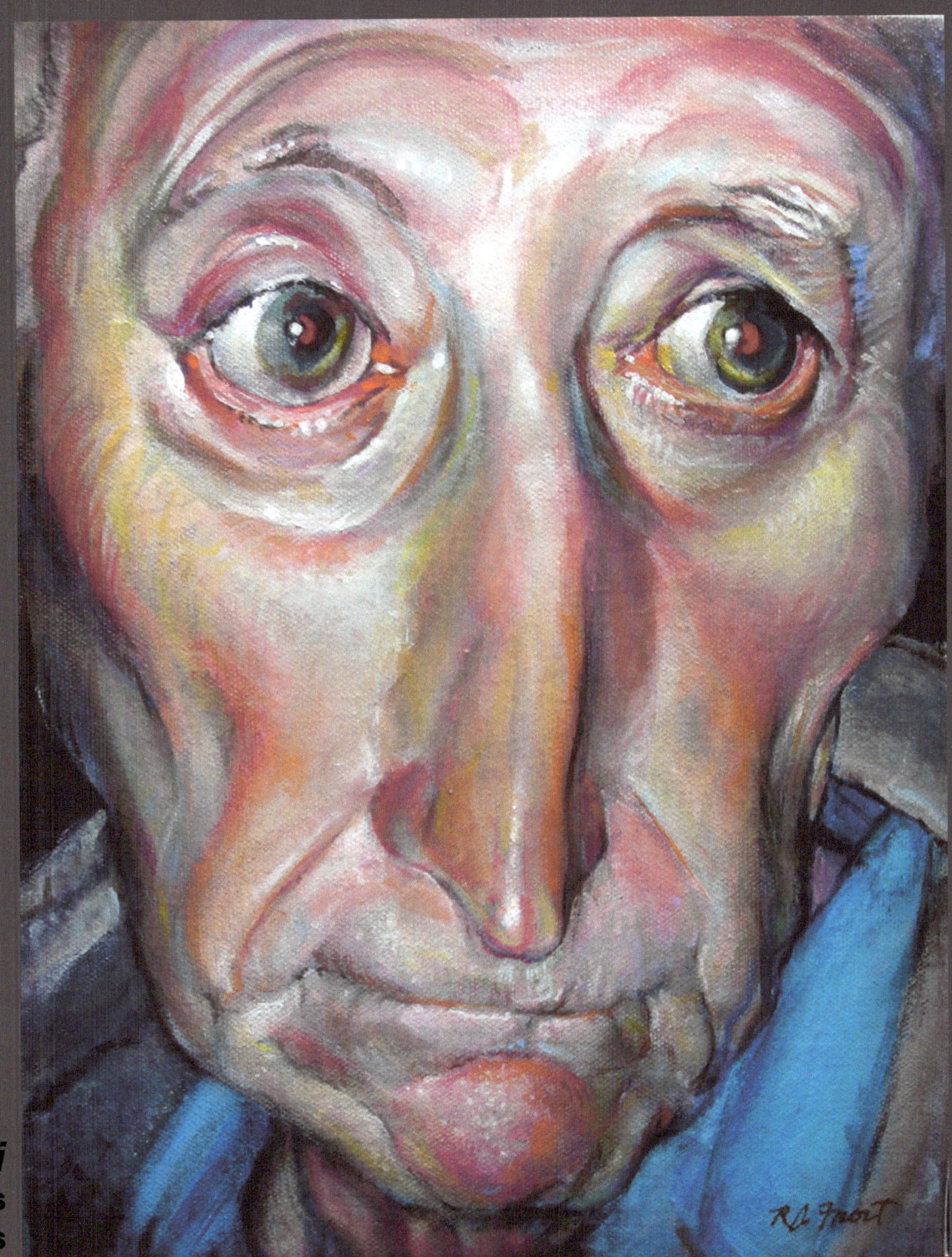

Richard Frost

Giovanni
Acrylic on canvas
9x12 inches

Artists Olga Shutova-Prashnova and Nikolay Prashnov are a couple who work from St. Petersburg, Russia.

Olga attended Repin State Academic Institute of Painting Sculpture and Architecture (Academy of Arts). She is also professional art critic and graphic artist.

Together they have been collaborating in painting, drawing, a long time were engaged in painting and a drawing, sculpture and doll making. They have participated in various art exhibitions since 2006. The dolls they co-create are porcelain and are and have aspects of surrealism.

www.sssdolls.com

ShirrStone Shelter

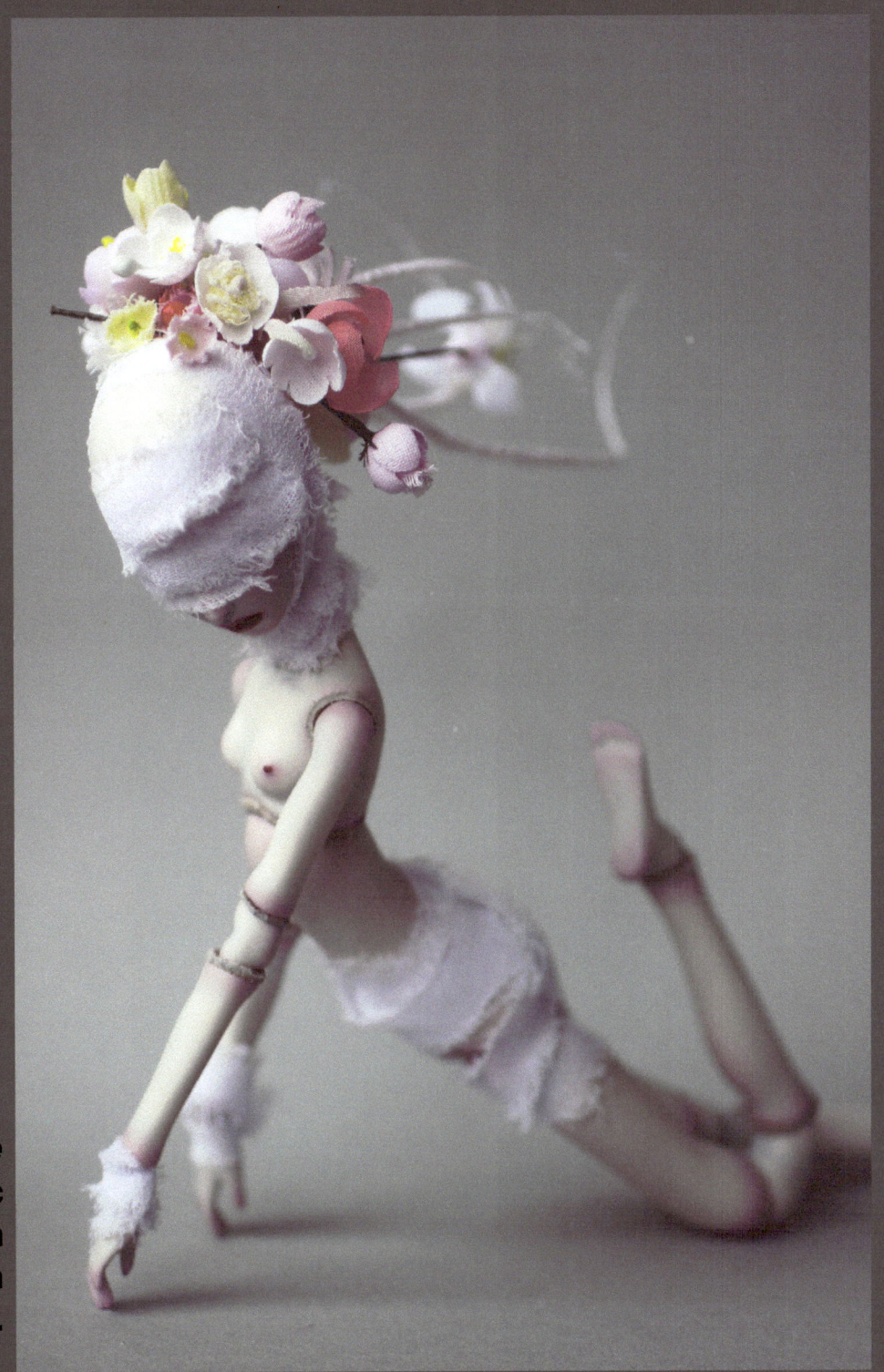

Albino Frozen Flame
**Psionic
Porcelain
H-29 cm
2013.**

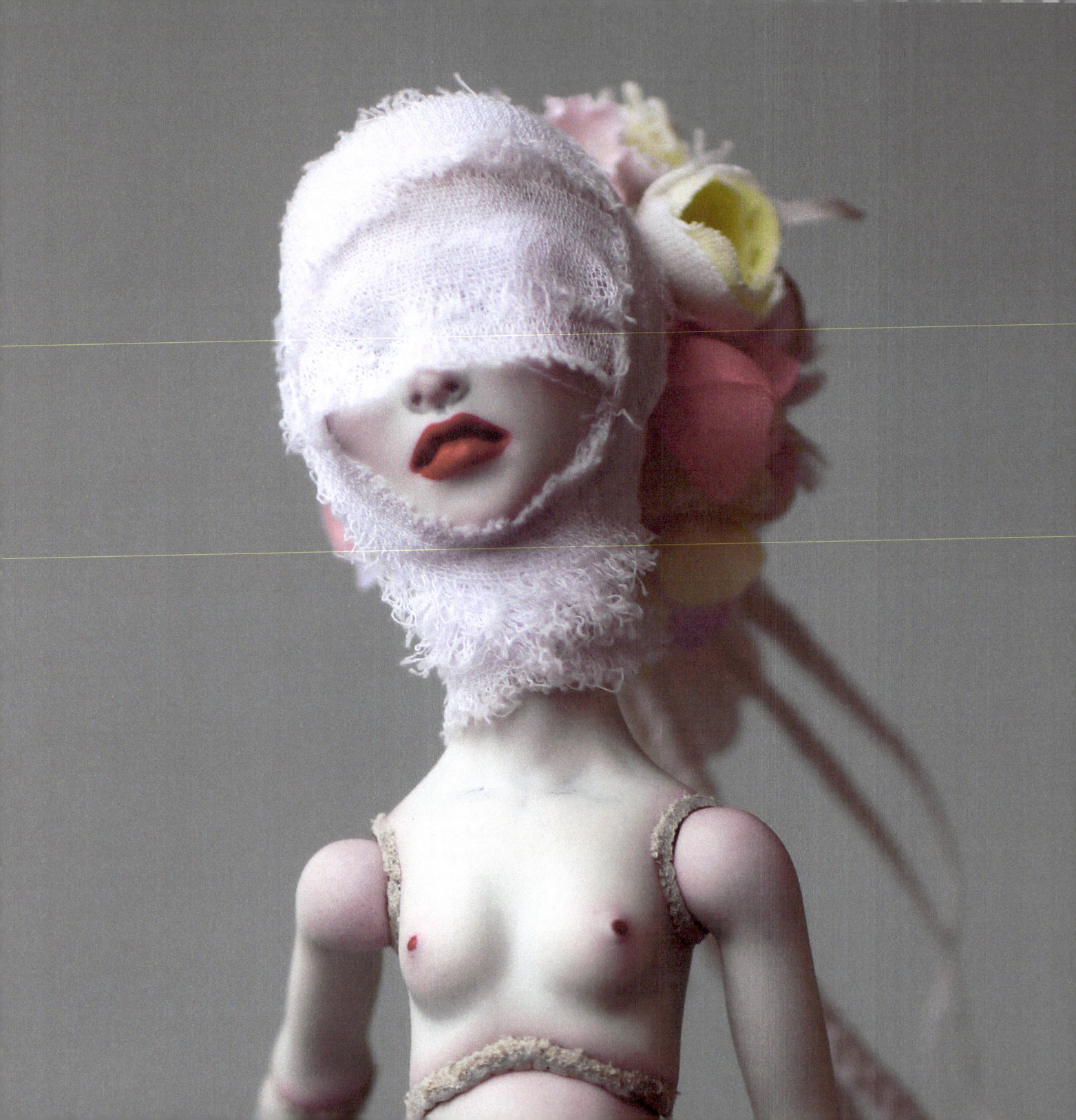

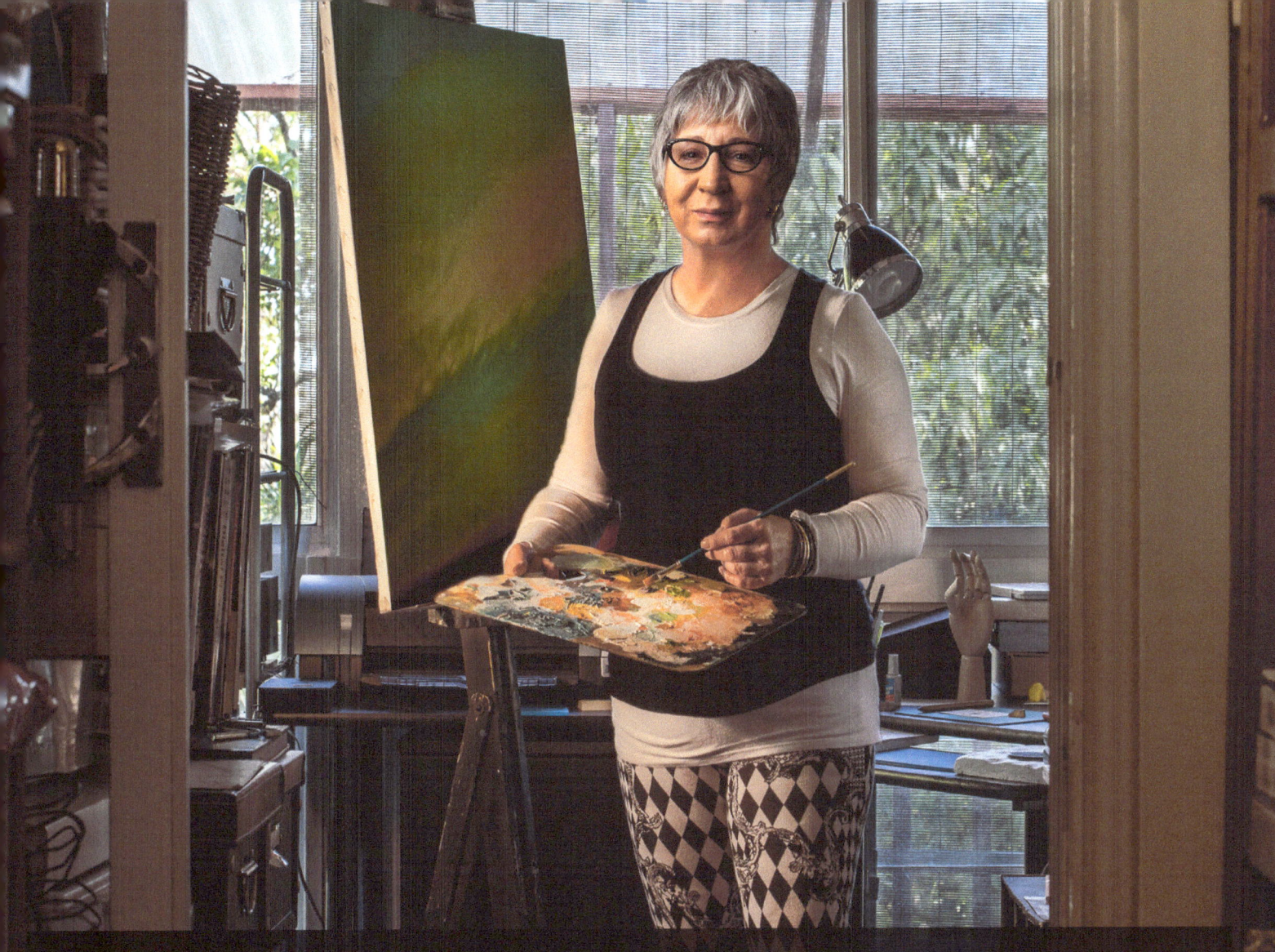

Raised on a farm near the southern coast of Tasmania, Debra Livingston grew up passionate about drawing from an early age. Farm life gave Debra plenty of subjects from animal life to dynamic scenery which to practice and hone her craft. Debra migrated at the age of 21, became involved in the art-scene in Sydney, New South Wales, Australia. She gained a Masters and a Doctorate in the visual arts, and resides on the north coast of Queensland. Debra lectures at the University of the Sunshine Coast, Queensland and has exhibited and sold her artworks from a very early age. In her arts practice she uses multi-mediums, pursuing photography, illustration and painting. Debra has solo and collaborative art exhibitions including international and national awards for her drawing and her photo-media being represented in public and private collections.

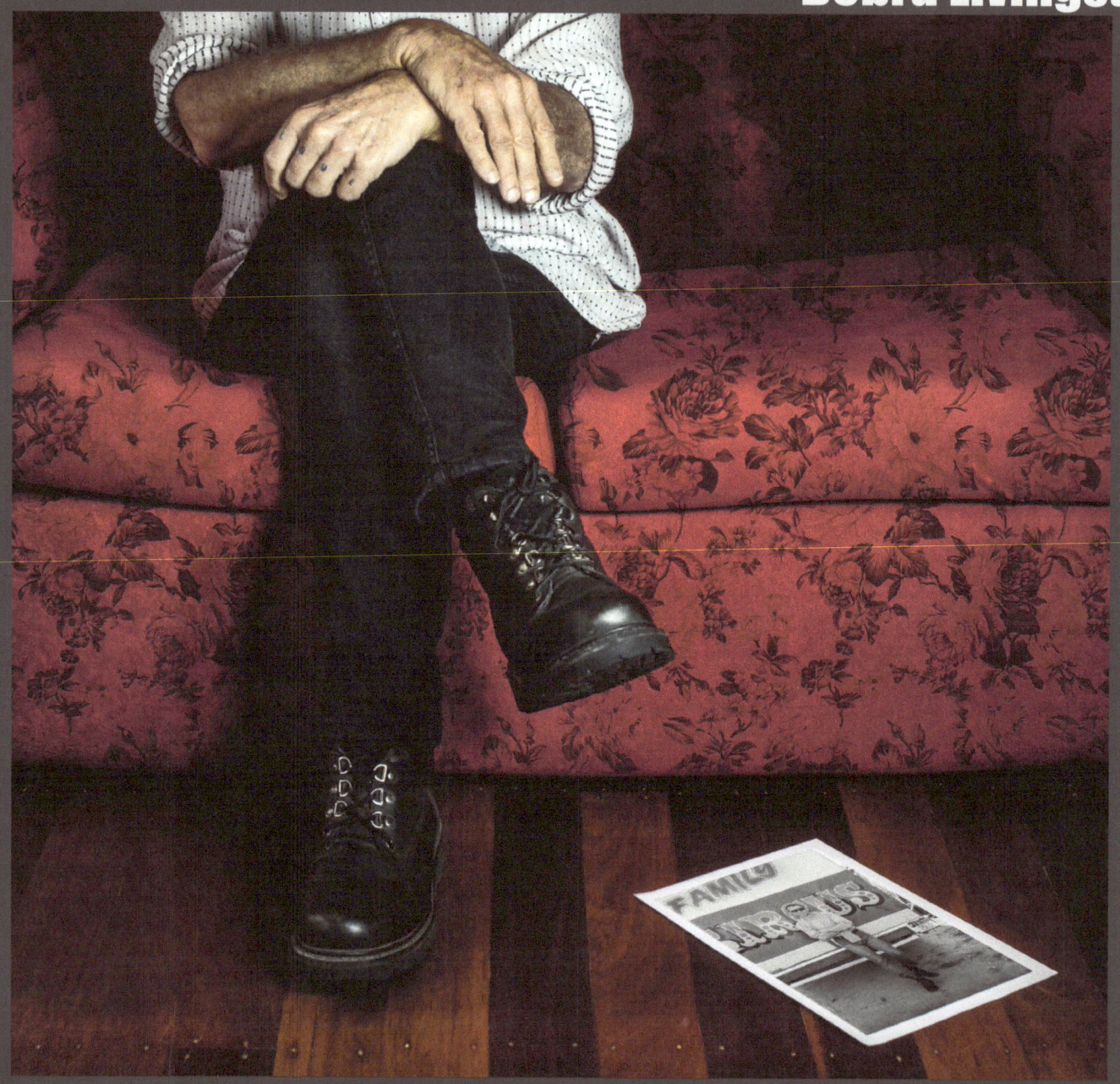

Debra Livingston

Looking back #2
PHOTOGRAPHY
21x30 cm

PA #55 Curated by Sergio Gomez May 2014

Jamilah Adebesin Mason

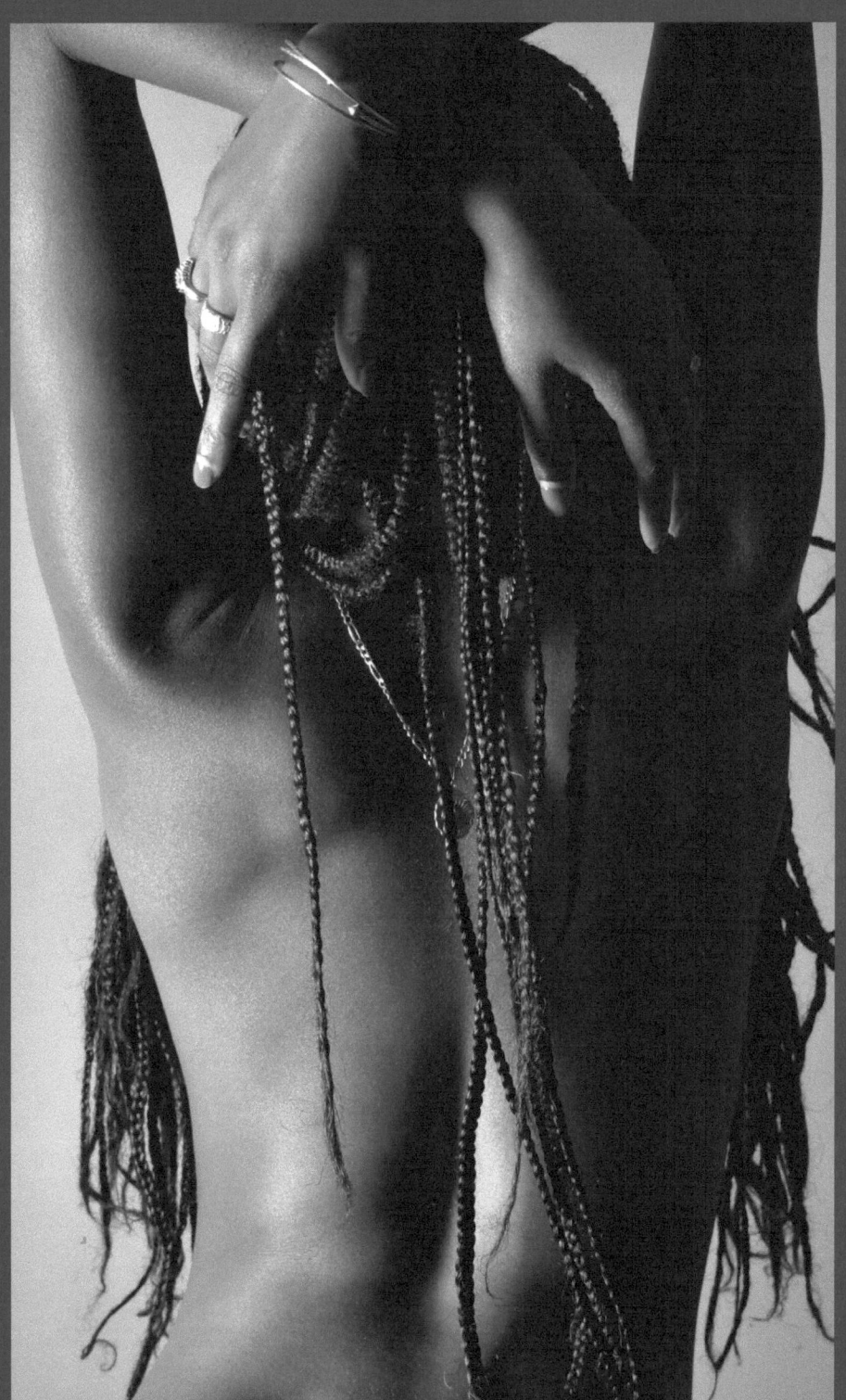

Raw
Digital Photography
2316px x 3849px

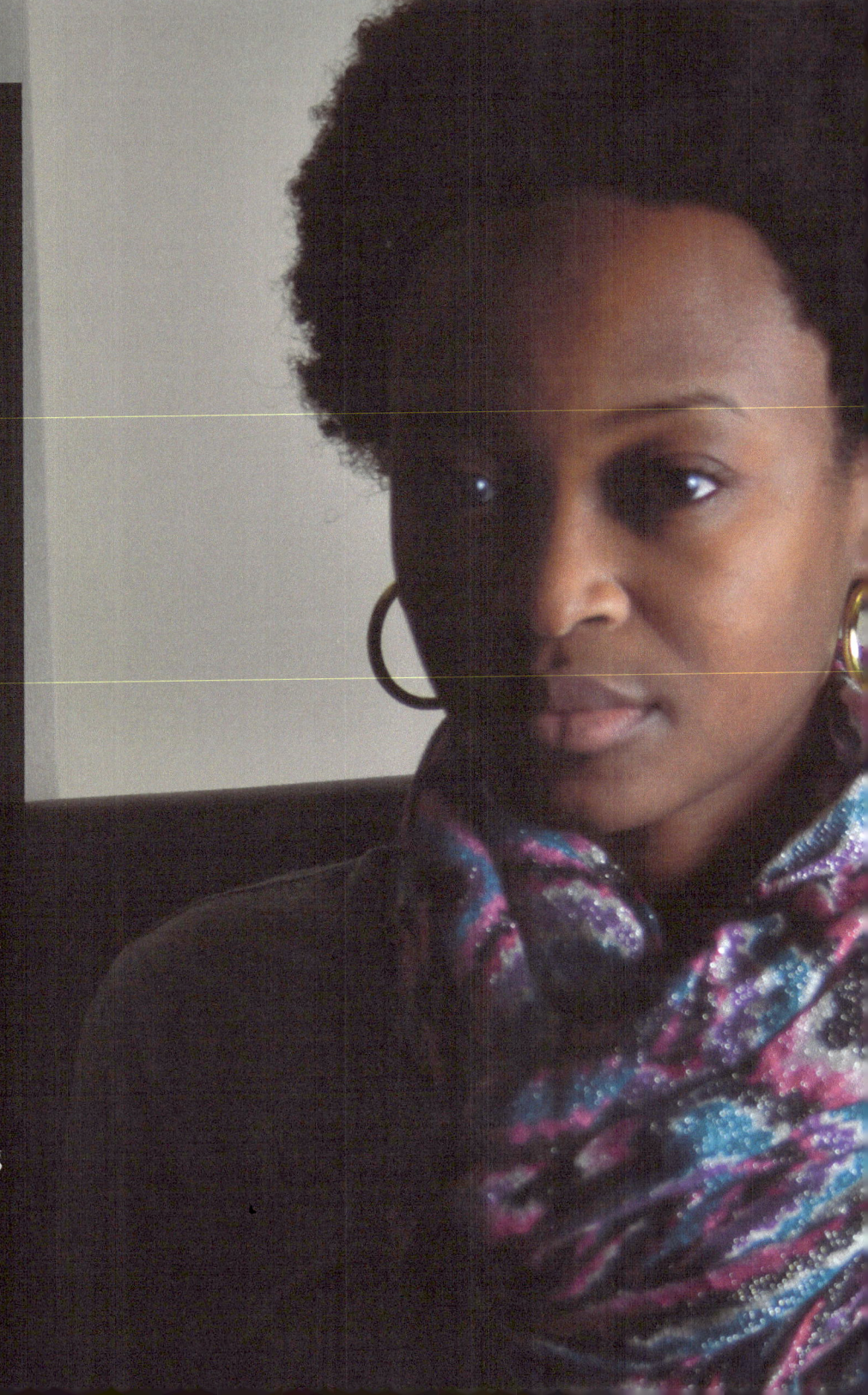

Jamilah Adebesin Mason was born on the South Side of Chicago to foreign born parents, Mukaila Adebesin of Nigeria, Africa and Wendy Mathurin Adebesin of Guyana, South America. Her love of art was apparent at a young age and was expressed through drawings of Disney characters and fashion illustrations. Her passion for the arts was encouraged through her father's love for journalism and her mother's love for interior design. Mason attained her Bachelor's of Fine Arts in Art Education at the University of Illinois at Chicago and recently received a Master's of Fine Arts in Digital Imaging and Independent Film from Governors State University. Mason is currently creating a body of work that serves as photographic journal entries. Her self portraits facilitate personal expression related to issues of racism, sexism, self sabotage, and personal fulfillment. Mason is currently a high school fine arts teacher and enjoys educating youth on the importance of the arts.

www.aworkofjam.com

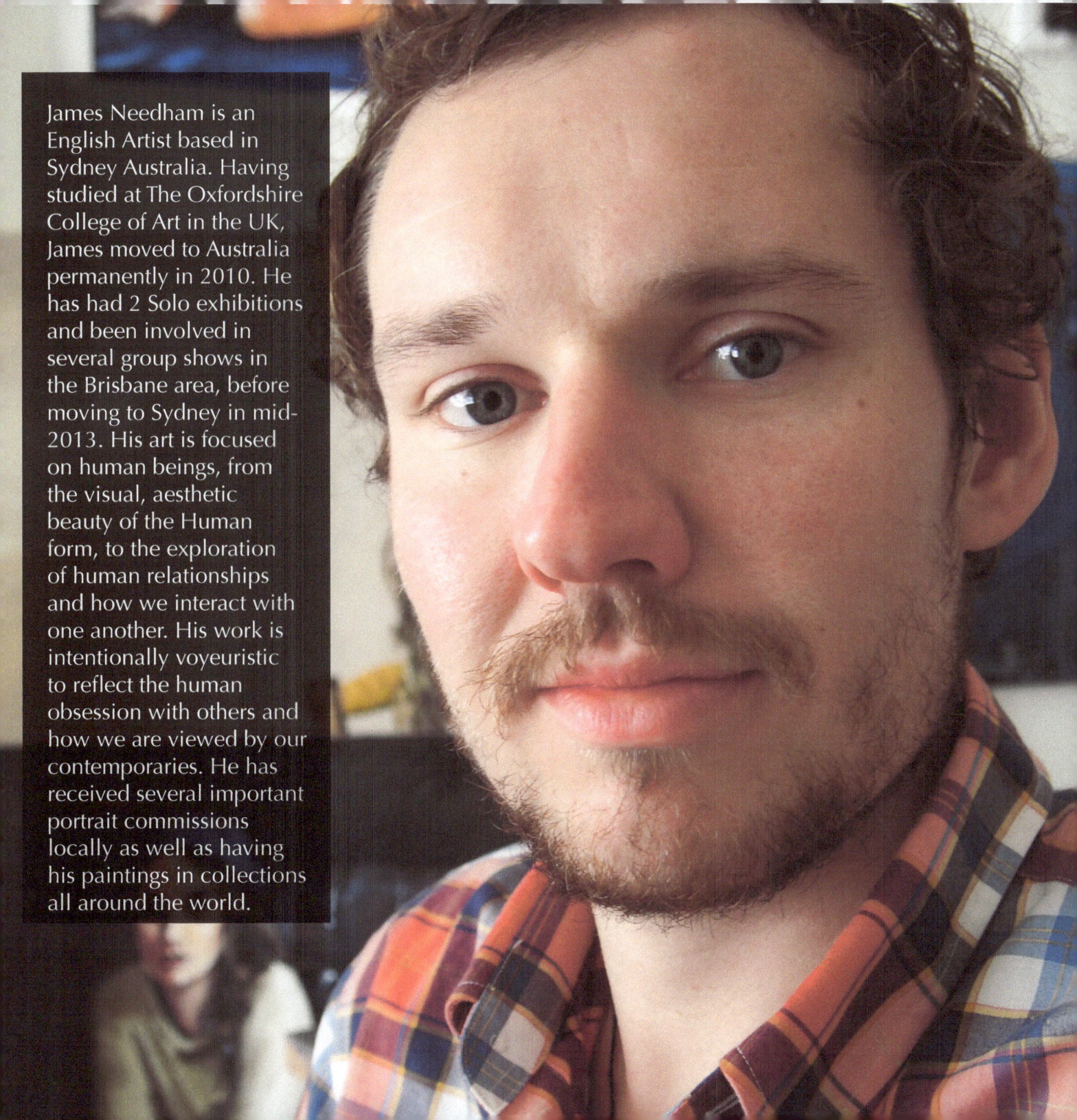

James Needham is an English Artist based in Sydney Australia. Having studied at The Oxfordshire College of Art in the UK, James moved to Australia permanently in 2010. He has had 2 Solo exhibitions and been involved in several group shows in the Brisbane area, before moving to Sydney in mid-2013. His art is focused on human beings, from the visual, aesthetic beauty of the Human form, to the exploration of human relationships and how we interact with one another. His work is intentionally voyeuristic to reflect the human obsession with others and how we are viewed by our contemporaries. He has received several important portrait commissions locally as well as having his paintings in collections all around the world.

James Needham

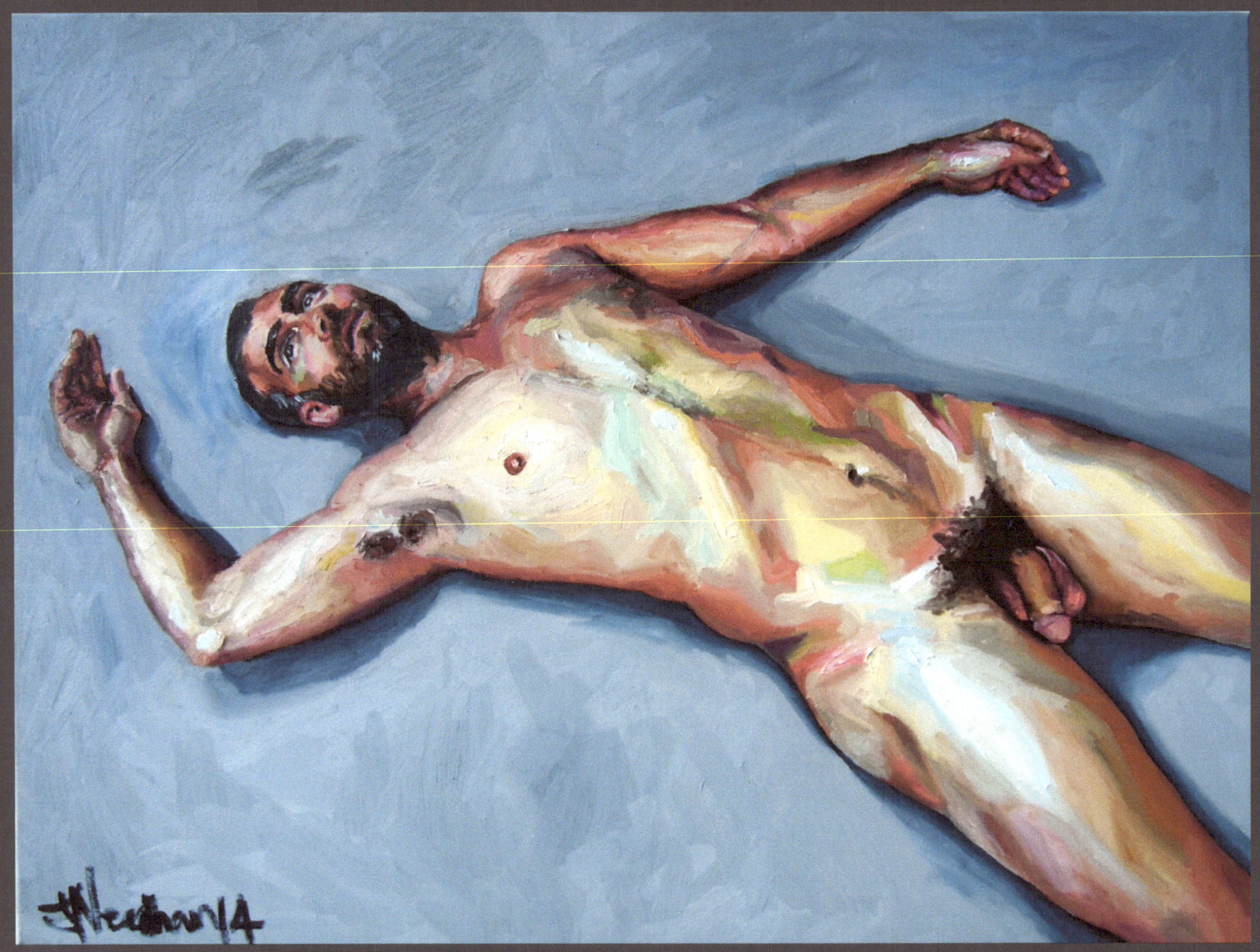

Luke
Oil on canvas
100 x 80 cm

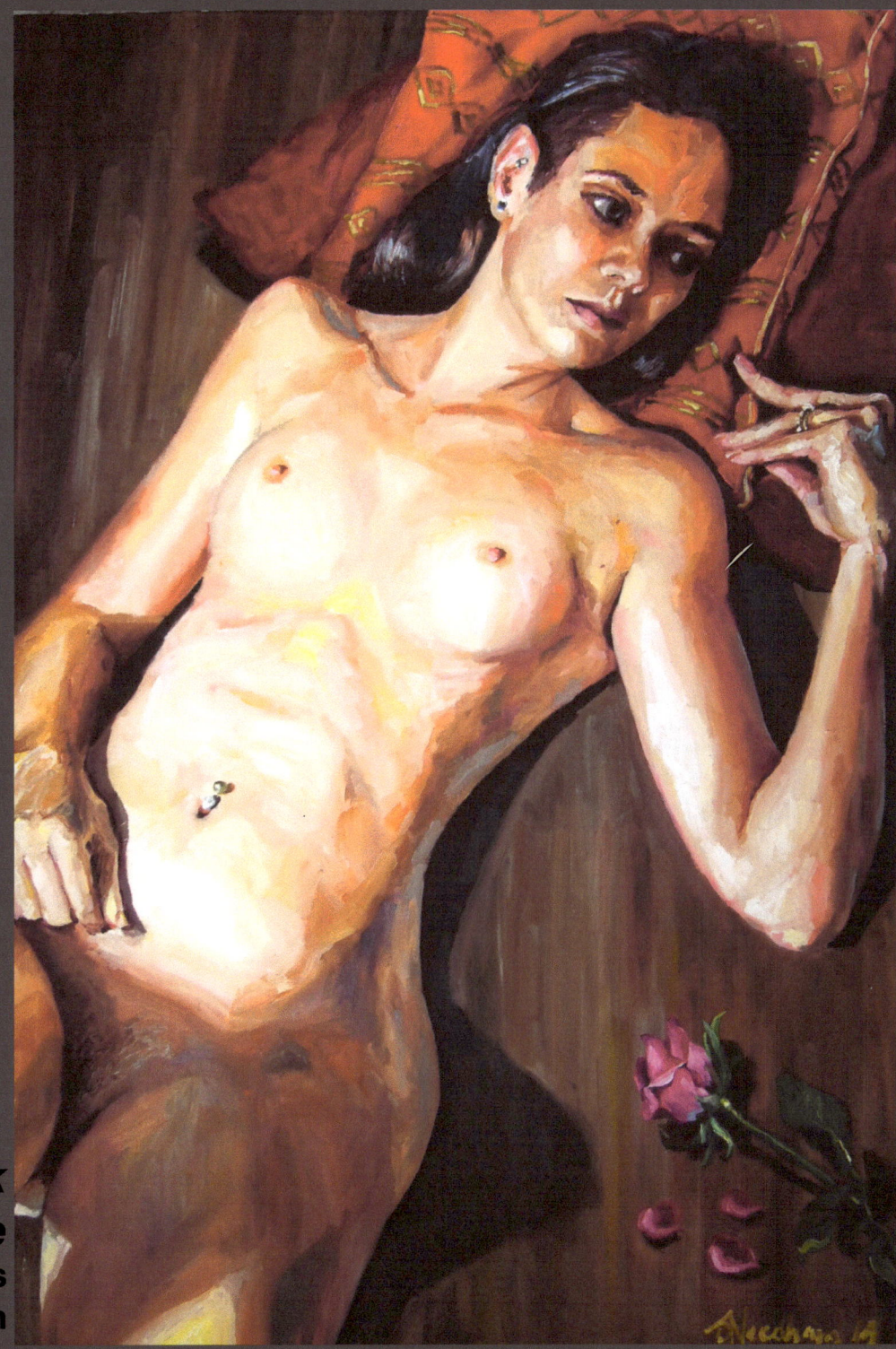

*Girl with Pink
Rose*
Oil on canvas
60 x 90 cm

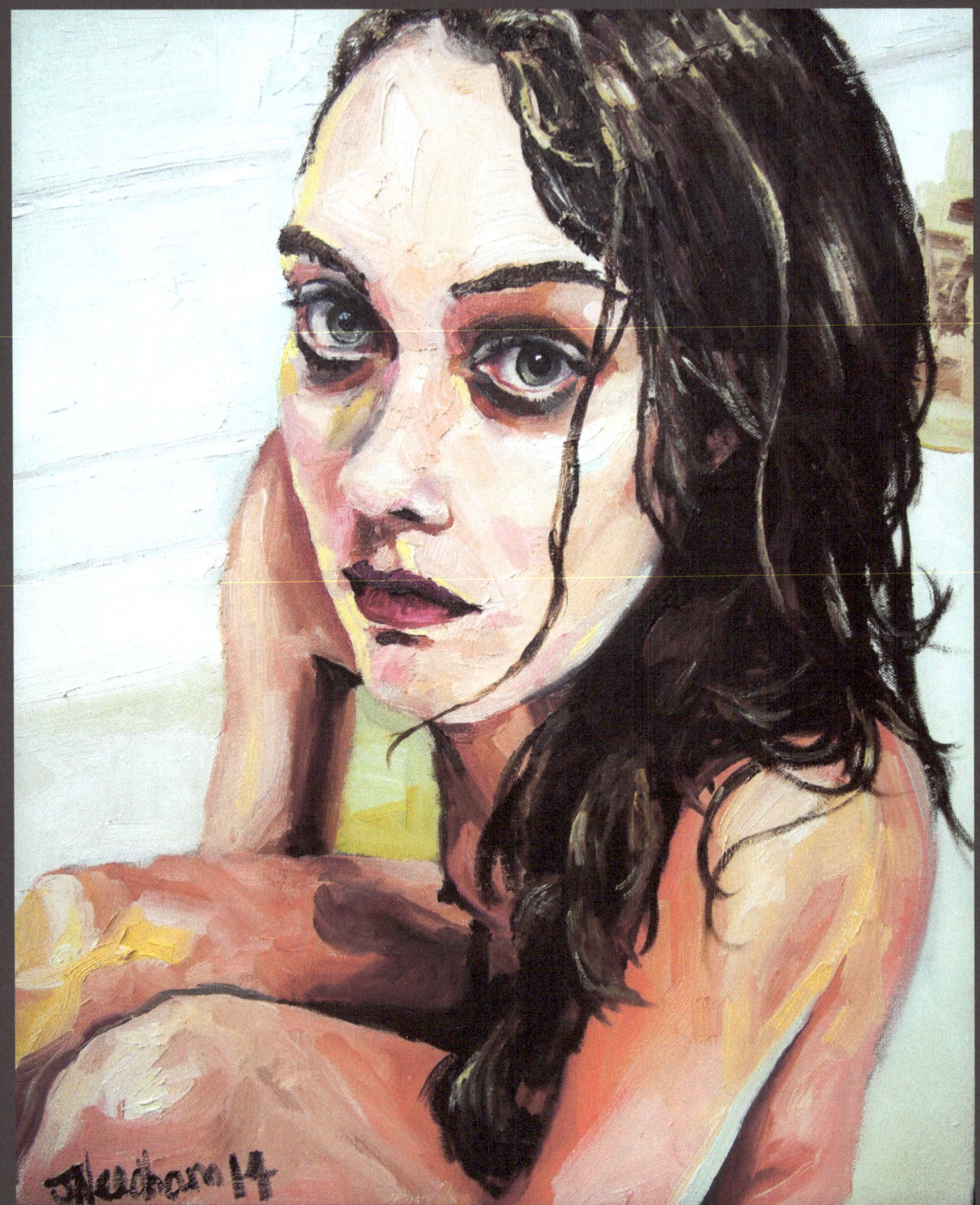

Bath
Oil on canvas
40 x 50cm